Linda Carrol
AF429756
SCAMMED
10 of the biggest current scams
and the
10 greatest of all time

Kindred Souls Press
Baytown, Texas 77520

Prologue: Unveiling Deception: The Greatest Scams of Today

Although there many scams out there today there will be even more in the future. There will always be those who want the easy money and don't care who it hurts. These are the current ones that are seeking easy prey.

Chapter 1: The Rise of Cryptocurrencies

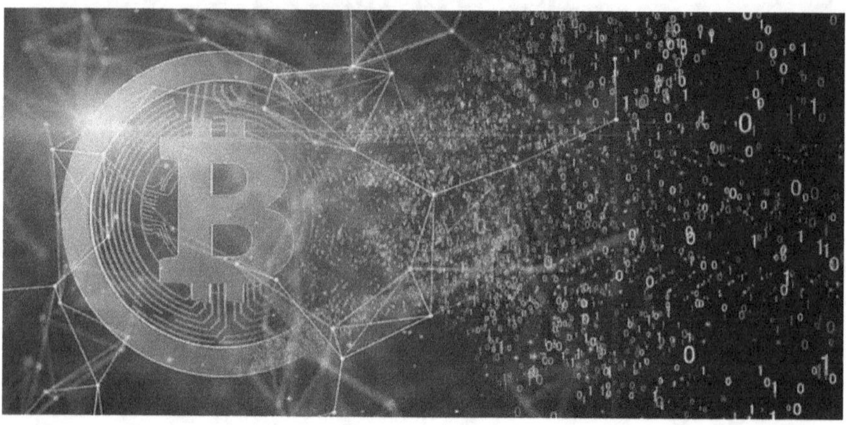

Cryptocurrencies have transformed the financial landscape since the inception of Bitcoin in 2009. Born out of the desire for a decentralized, secure form of digital currency, cryptocurrencies have captivated the world. However, along with their rise, there has been a significant increase in scams aimed at exploiting both novice and seasoned investors. Understanding the evolution of these digital assets is crucial to appreciating the complexities of the scams that have emerged alongside them.

The Birth of Bitcoin

Bitcoin, the first cryptocurrency, was introduced by an anonymous person or group of people using the pseudonym Satoshi Nakamoto. The release of the Bitcoin whitepaper in 2008 outlined a peer-to-peer electronic cash system that eliminated the need for intermediaries like banks. Bitcoin's decentralized nature, secured by cryptographic principles and blockchain technology, was revolutionary.

The Emergence of Altcoins

Following Bitcoin's success, numerous alternative cryptocurrencies, known as altcoins, began to emerge. Ethereum, launched in 2015, introduced smart contracts, further expanding the possibilities of blockchain technology. These developments spurred a wave of innovation and investment, making the cryptocurrency market a lucrative target for scammers.

Rapid Market Growth

The cryptocurrency market saw exponential growth, with prices of Bitcoin and other digital assets reaching unprecedented heights. This growth attracted a diverse group of investors, many of whom were new to the world of finance and technology. Unfortunately, this influx also drew the attention of scammers looking to exploit the booming market.

Media coverage and celebrity endorsements have played significant roles in popularizing cryptocurrencies. High-profile endorsements, however, have sometimes led to the promotion of fraudulent schemes. Understanding the influence of media and celebrity endorsements is crucial in comprehending the dynamics of cryptocurrency scams.

Cryptocurrencies, with their promise of anonymity and decentralized control, have revolutionized the financial landscape. However, these same characteristics make them a fertile ground for scammers. Understanding why cryptocurrencies are so attractive to fraudsters is essential in recognizing and avoiding potential scams.

One of the core features of cryptocurrencies is the ability to conduct transactions with a high degree of privacy. Unlike traditional banking systems, which require personal identification, cryptocurrency transactions can be conducted pseudonymously. This anonymity makes it difficult to trace transactions back to individuals, providing a shield for scammers to operate under the radar.

The cryptocurrency market operates in a relatively unregulated environment. While some countries have started to implement regulations, the global nature of cryptocurrencies means that they often fall outside the jurisdiction of any single regulatory body. This lack of oversight makes it easier for scammers to perpetrate fraud without facing immediate legal consequences.

Cryptocurrencies are known for their price volatility, with values that can skyrocket or plummet within a short period. This volatility attracts both legitimate investors seeking high returns and scammers looking to exploit the market's unpredictability. Scammers often use promises of guaranteed high returns to lure unsuspecting victims.

The decentralized nature of cryptocurrencies means there is no central authority to oversee transactions or step in to reverse fraudulent activities. This decentralization is a double-edged sword: while it provides freedom from traditional financial institutions, it also leaves users vulnerable to scams with little recourse for recovery.

The technology underpinning cryptocurrencies, including blockchain and cryptographic algorithms, can be complex and difficult for the average person to understand. Scammers exploit this complexity, creating schemes that appear legitimate but are actually designed to deceive those who lack technical knowledge.

Case Study: The QuadrigaCX Collapse

QuadrigaCX was a Canadian cryptocurrency exchange that collapsed in 2019, leaving thousands of investors unable to access their funds. The founder, Gerald Cotten, reportedly died suddenly, taking the private keys needed to access the exchange's wallets to his grave. Subsequent investigations revealed that the exchange had been operating as a Ponzi scheme, with Cotten using customer funds for personal gain. The lack of regulatory oversight and the complexity of the technology used by QuadrigaCX made it an attractive target for scammers and a devastating blow to its users.

As the cryptocurrency market began to take shape, it didn't take long for scammers to recognize the potential for fraudulent schemes. Early scams laid the groundwork for more sophisticated frauds that would follow. By examining these early incidents, we can learn valuable lessons about the tactics scammers use and the vulnerabilities they exploit.

In the early days of Bitcoin, scams were relatively unsophisticated but still effective. Common tactics included fake exchanges, phishing attacks, and Ponzi schemes. These scams preyed on the lack of knowledge and experience among early adopters.

Case Study: Bitcoin Savings & Trust

Bitcoin Savings & Trust, operated by Trendon Shavers, was one of the first major Ponzi schemes in the cryptocurrency space. Promising weekly returns of up to 7%, Shavers attracted over $4.5 million worth of Bitcoin from investors. In reality, he was using new investments to pay returns to earlier investors while pocketing significant amounts for himself. When the scheme collapsed in 2012, many investors were left with significant losses.

The Mt. Gox Hack

Mt. Gox was once the largest Bitcoin exchange, handling over 70% of all Bitcoin transactions worldwide. In 2014, the exchange filed for bankruptcy after it was revealed that 850,000 Bitcoins had been stolen, likely due to a series of hacks over several years. The incident highlighted the importance of security in cryptocurrency exchanges and the devastating impact that a major breach could have on the market and individual investors.

Case Study: Silk Road

Silk Road was an online black market that used Bitcoin for transactions. While it wasn't a scam in the traditional sense, it played a significant role in the early association between Bitcoin and illicit activities. The site was eventually shut down by the FBI in 2013, and its founder, Ross Ulbricht, was sentenced to life in prison. Silk Road's existence and eventual downfall drew significant attention to the risks and regulatory challenges associated with cryptocurrencies.

The early scams in the cryptocurrency market taught several important lessons:

Importance of Security: The Mt. Gox hack underscored the need for robust security measures to protect digital assets.

Regulatory Oversight: Incidents like Bitcoin Savings & Trust and Silk Road highlighted the need for regulatory oversight to protect investors and combat illicit activities.

Investor Education: The success of early scams was largely due to the lack of knowledge among investors. As the market matures, education becomes crucial in helping investors make informed decisions.

As cryptocurrencies gained mainstream attention, the scale and sophistication of scams also increased. This chapter delves into some of the most infamous cryptocurrency scams, examining how they operated, their impact on victims, and the lessons learned from each case.

OneCoin

OneCoin, launched in 2014 by Ruja Ignatova, was marketed as a revolutionary cryptocurrency that would surpass Bitcoin. In reality, it was a massive Ponzi scheme. Ignatova and her team promised investors high returns and recruited new members through a multi-level marketing structure. By the time authorities intervened, OneCoin had defrauded investors of over $4 billion. Ignatova disappeared in 2017 and remains at large, earning her the nickname "Cryptoqueen."

Case Study: BitConnect

BitConnect was a cryptocurrency lending platform that promised high returns through a proprietary trading bot and volatility software. Launched in 2016, BitConnect quickly gained popularity, with its token (BCC) reaching a market cap of over $2.5 billion. However, in 2018, the platform was shut down following cease-and-desist orders from regulators, and it was revealed to be a Ponzi scheme. Investors lost millions as the value of BCC plummeted to near zero.

The PlusToken Scam

PlusToken was a high-yield investment program (HYIP) that targeted Asian investors, promising returns of up to 30% per month. Launched in 2018, PlusToken attracted over $3 billion from investors. In 2019, the scam unraveled when key members of the team were arrested, and it was revealed that the operators had been siphoning off funds. The aftermath of the PlusToken scam led to significant sell-offs in the cryptocurrency market, affecting prices across the board.

The Centra Tech ICO

Centra Tech conducted an initial coin offering (ICO) in 2017, raising over $25 million by promising a range of financial products, including a cryptocurrency debit card. The ICO was heavily promoted by celebrities like Floyd Mayweather and DJ Khaled. However, it was later revealed that the founders had fabricated partnerships and lied about the capabilities of their products. The founders were arrested in 2018, and investors faced significant losses.

The Case of Bitfinex and Tether

While not a traditional scam, the relationship between the cryptocurrency exchange Bitfinex and the stablecoin Tether (USDT) has been controversial. In 2019, the New York Attorney General accused Bitfinex of using Tether funds to cover up $850 million in losses. The case raised concerns about the transparency and backing of Tether, which is supposed to be pegged to the US dollar. The ongoing legal battles and investigations continue to cast a shadow over the cryptocurrency market.

Lessons from Famous Scams

Due Diligence: Investors must conduct thorough research and due diligence before investing in any cryptocurrency or platform.

Regulatory Signals: Pay attention to warnings and actions from regulatory bodies, as they often indicate underlying issues.

Diversification: Avoid putting all investments into a single cryptocurrency or platform to mitigate risks.

Scammers in the cryptocurrency space are constantly evolving their tactics. However, there are common red flags and patterns that can help investors identify potential scams. This chapter provides practical tips and strategies for spotting and avoiding fraudulent schemes.

Common Red Flags

Unrealistic Promises: Scams often promise guaranteed high returns with little or no risk. Be wary of any investment that sounds too good to be true.

Lack of Transparency: Legitimate projects are usually transparent about their team, technology, and business model. If a project lacks detailed information or the team members are anonymous, it's a red flag.

Pressure Tactics: Scammers often use high-pressure tactics to rush investors into making decisions without adequate time to research.

Complex or Vague Explanations: If the technology or business model is overly complex or vague and difficult to understand, it could be a sign of a scam.

Phishing and Social Engineering

Phishing and social engineering attacks are common in the cryptocurrency space. Scammers often impersonate legitimate companies or individuals to trick victims into revealing their private keys or login credentials. Always verify the authenticity of communications and avoid clicking on suspicious links.

Fake Exchanges and Wallets

Scammers create fake cryptocurrency exchanges and wallets to steal funds. Ensure that any exchange or wallet you use is reputable and has positive reviews from the community.

Ponzi and Pyramid Schemes

Ponzi and pyramid schemes rely on new investments to pay returns to earlier investors. Be cautious of any investment that requires recruiting new members or promises returns from new investments rather than actual business activities.

Case Study: The BitClub Network

The BitClub Network was a mining pool that operated from 2014 to 2019, promising high returns through cryptocurrency mining. In reality, it was a Ponzi scheme that defrauded investors of over $722 million. The operators used fake mining earnings to lure in new investors while using funds from new members to pay returns to earlier investors. The scheme unraveled when the operators were arrested, highlighting the importance of skepticism and due diligence.

Tools and Resources

Blockchain Explorers: Use blockchain explorers to verify transactions and the legitimacy of a project's claims.

Community Reviews: Check forums, social media, and review sites for community feedback on a project.

Regulatory Warnings: Stay informed about warnings and alerts from regulatory bodies regarding specific projects or platforms.

While the risk of scams cannot be entirely eliminated, there are several strategies and best practices that investors can use to protect themselves. This chapter outlines practical steps for safeguarding investments in the cryptocurrency space.

Secure Your Investments

Use Hardware Wallets: Hardware wallets provide a high level of security by keeping private keys offline. They are less susceptible to hacking and phishing attacks.

Enable Two-Factor Authentication (2FA): Enable 2FA on all cryptocurrency accounts to add an extra layer of security.

Regular Backups: Regularly backup your wallet and store the backup in a secure location.

Conduct Thorough Research

Whitepapers and Roadmaps: Review the project's whitepaper and roadmap to understand its goals, technology, and timeline. Be wary of projects with vague or unrealistic plans.

Team and Advisors: Research the team members and advisors behind the project. Verify their identities and professional backgrounds.

Community Engagement: Active and engaged communities are often a sign of a legitimate project. Participate in forums and social media groups to gauge the community's sentiment and activity.

Diversify Your Portfolio

Diversifying your cryptocurrency investments can mitigate risks. Avoid putting all your funds into a single project or asset. Spread your investments across different types of cryptocurrencies and projects.

Stay Informed

The cryptocurrency market is constantly evolving. Stay informed about the latest news, regulatory changes, and emerging threats. Subscribe to reputable cryptocurrency news sources and follow industry experts on social media.

Case Study: The Safeguard of Cold Storage

Cold storage refers to keeping cryptocurrencies offline, away from internet access. This method is highly secure and protects against online hacking attempts. A notable example is the Winklevoss twins, who reportedly store their Bitcoin in multiple pieces of paper spread across different physical locations. This extreme measure highlights the importance of security and the lengths some investors go to protect their assets.

The legal and regulatory landscape for cryptocurrencies is rapidly evolving. Governments and regulatory bodies around the world are taking steps to address the challenges and risks associated with digital assets. This chapter explores the current state of regulation and its impact on preventing cryptocurrency scams.

Regulatory Approaches

United States: The U.S. has taken a proactive approach, with agencies like the SEC and CFTC playing significant roles in regulating cryptocurrencies. Recent actions include prosecuting fraudulent ICOs and enforcing anti-money laundering (AML) regulations.

European Union: The EU has implemented the Fifth Anti-Money Laundering Directive (5AMLD), which includes regulations for cryptocurrency exchanges and wallet providers. The EU is also working on a comprehensive framework for digital assets.

Asia: Countries like Japan and South Korea have established robust regulatory frameworks, requiring exchanges to register and comply with AML and KYC (Know Your Customer) regulations. China, on the other hand, has banned cryptocurrency trading and ICOs altogether.

The Role of Self-Regulation

In addition to government regulations, the cryptocurrency industry has seen the emergence of self-regulatory organizations (SROs). These organizations set industry standards and best practices, helping to enhance security and trust within the market. Examples include the Japan Virtual Currency Exchange Association (JVCEA) and the CryptoUK.

Challenges in Regulation

Global Nature of Cryptocurrencies: Cryptocurrencies operate on a global scale, making it difficult for any single country to regulate effectively. This creates opportunities for regulatory arbitrage, where scammers exploit jurisdictions with lax regulations.

Rapid Technological Advancements: The fast-paced development of blockchain technology often outstrips the ability of regulators to keep up. This can lead to gaps in oversight and enforcement.

Balancing Innovation and Protection: Regulators face the challenge of balancing the need to protect investors with the desire to foster innovation. Overly restrictive regulations could stifle the growth of legitimate projects and the broader cryptocurrency market.

Case Study: The Impact of Regulation on ICOs

Initial Coin Offerings (ICOs) were a popular fundraising method during the cryptocurrency boom of 2017. However, the lack of regulation led to numerous scams and fraudulent projects. In response, regulatory bodies like the SEC began cracking down on ICOs, classifying many as securities and enforcing strict compliance requirements. This regulatory intervention significantly reduced the number of ICOs and helped to restore some investor confidence.

As cryptocurrencies continue to evolve, so too will the tactics and strategies employed by scammers. This chapter explores potential future trends in cryptocurrency scams and how investors can stay vigilant.

Emerging Technologies and Scams

DeFi (Decentralized Finance): DeFi platforms, which offer decentralized financial services, have become a new target for scammers. Rug pulls, where developers abandon a project and run off with investors' funds, are a common threat in the DeFi space.

NFTs (Non-Fungible Tokens): NFTs have gained popularity for their ability to represent unique digital assets. However, the hype around NFTs has also attracted scammers who create and sell fake or plagiarized tokens.

Quantum Computing: The advent of quantum computing poses a potential threat to the cryptographic algorithms that secure cryptocurrencies. While practical quantum computers are still years away, the industry must prepare for the possibility of future vulnerabilities.

AI and machine learning can both aid and combat cryptocurrency scams. Scammers may use AI to create more convincing phishing attacks and social engineering schemes. On the flip side, these technologies can also be used to detect and prevent fraudulent activities by analyzing transaction patterns and identifying anomalies.

Increasing Regulation and Compliance

As regulatory frameworks become more sophisticated, scammers will likely adapt by finding new ways to circumvent regulations. However, increased collaboration between regulatory bodies, industry players, and technology providers can help to enhance security and reduce the prevalence of scams.

Educating the Next Generation of Investors

Education remains one of the most effective tools in combating cryptocurrency scams. As more people become interested in digital assets, it is crucial to provide resources and training to help them understand the risks and how to protect themselves. Initiatives like blockchain education programs and online courses can play a significant role in raising awareness.

Case Study: The Role of Blockchain Analytics

Blockchain analytics companies like Chainalysis and CipherTrace use advanced algorithms to track and analyze cryptocurrency transactions. These tools can help law enforcement agencies identify and apprehend scammers by tracing the flow of funds across the blockchain. The increasing use of blockchain analytics demonstrates the potential for technology to combat fraud and enhance transparency in the cryptocurrency market.

Cryptocurrencies have revolutionized the financial landscape, offering new opportunities and challenges. While the promise of decentralization and digital assets is exciting, it also comes with significant risks, particularly from scams. By understanding the history of cryptocurrency scams, recognizing red flags, and adopting best practices for security, investors can navigate this complex market more safely.

As the cryptocurrency market continues to grow and evolve, staying informed and vigilant is more important than ever. By learning from past scams and anticipating future threats, we can protect our investments and contribute to a safer and more transparent financial ecosystem.

Chapter 2: Phishing Scams

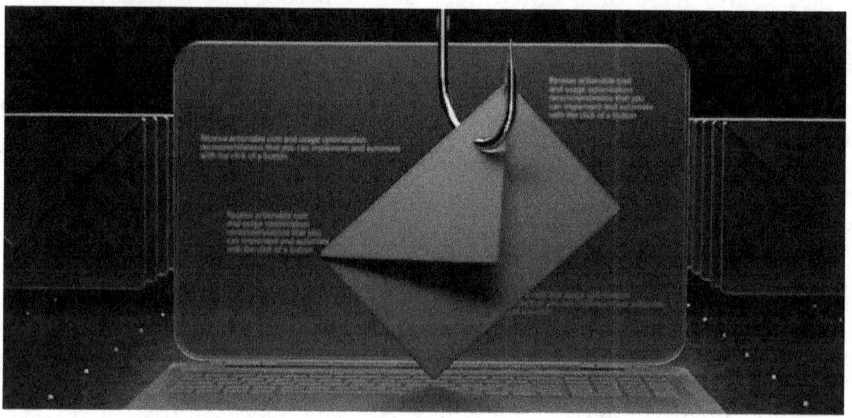

Phishing scams have been a persistent threat since the early days of the internet. The term "phishing" itself is a play on the word "fishing," where attackers use bait to catch their victims. Phishing typically involves tricking individuals into providing sensitive information, such as usernames, passwords, and credit card details, by masquerading as a trustworthy entity.

The history of phishing can be traced back to the 1990s. One of the earliest and most notable instances occurred in the mid-1990s with the rise of America Online (AOL). Cybercriminals would pose as AOL employees, sending messages to users asking for their login credentials. Many unsuspecting users fell for these tricks, leading to significant account breaches.

As technology advanced, so did phishing techniques. In the early 2000s, phishing scams began to target online payment systems and e-commerce platforms. The infamous eBay phishing scam of 2003 saw fraudsters sending fake emails purportedly from eBay, directing users to a bogus website to enter their login information. This scam affected thousands of users and highlighted the growing sophistication of phishing attacks.

Phishing continued to evolve, incorporating new methods such as spear phishing and clone phishing. Spear phishing targets specific individuals or organizations, often using personal information to make the scam more convincing. Clone phishing involves duplicating a legitimate email and altering it slightly to include malicious links or attachments.

One of the most significant milestones in the history of phishing was the introduction of ransomware in phishing emails. Ransomware encrypts the victim's data and demands payment for the decryption key. This type of attack became widespread in the 2010s, causing significant financial losses and data breaches.

Overall, the history of phishing scams demonstrates a continual adaptation and sophistication in techniques, making it crucial for individuals and organizations to stay informed and vigilant.

Case Study 1: AOL Phishing Scam (1995)

In 1995, AOL was a dominant player in the internet service provider market, and with millions of users, it became a prime target for phishing attacks. Cybercriminals would send messages to AOL users, pretending to be AOL employees and asking for their passwords. The messages often included threats of account termination if the information was not provided. Many users, fearing the loss of their accounts, fell victim to these scams, resulting in compromised accounts and financial losses.

The impact of the AOL phishing scam was significant, leading to increased awareness and the implementation of stricter security measures by AOL. This case highlighted the need for better user education on recognizing and avoiding phishing attempts.

Case Study 2: The eBay Scam (2003)

In 2003, eBay users became the targets of a sophisticated phishing scam. Fraudsters sent emails that appeared to be from eBay, informing users of suspicious activity on their accounts and urging them to click on a link to verify their information. The link led to a fake eBay login page designed to steal user credentials. Thousands of eBay users were affected, resulting in unauthorized access to their accounts and financial losses.

This scam underscored the importance of verifying the authenticity of emails and websites before entering sensitive information. eBay responded by enhancing its security measures and educating users on how to identify phishing emails.

Case Study 3: The Sony PlayStation Network Phishing (2011)

In 2011, Sony's PlayStation Network (PSN) experienced a major phishing attack that compromised the personal information of approximately 77 million accounts. Hackers sent phishing emails to PSN users, luring them to fake websites to input their login credentials. Once the hackers had access to the accounts, they exploited personal data, including credit card information.

The PSN phishing scam had far-reaching consequences, including financial losses for users and a significant blow to Sony's reputation. It prompted Sony to enhance its security infrastructure and implement more rigorous authentication processes.

Phishing scams can be devastating, but with the right knowledge and precautions, you can protect yourself. Here are some essential tips to avoid falling victim to phishing scams:

Recognizing Phishing Emails

Phishing emails often have telltale signs:

Unfamiliar sender addresses or spoofed email addresses

Urgent or threatening language, such as "Your account will be suspended"

Requests for personal information, passwords, or financial details

Poor grammar and spelling mistakes

Suspicious links or attachments

Adopting safe browsing habits can significantly reduce your risk of phishing attacks:

Always verify the URL of websites before entering personal information

Look for secure connections (HTTPS) and the padlock icon in the browser address bar

Avoid clicking on links or downloading attachments from unknown sources

Regularly update your web browser and security software

Tools and Technologies to Protect Yourself

Utilize tools and technologies designed to enhance your online security:

Install and maintain reputable antivirus software to detect and block phishing attempts

Use browser extensions that provide warnings about suspicious websites

Enable two-factor authentication (2FA) for an extra layer of security on your accounts

Real-Life Case Studies

Case Study 1: Target Corporation Data Breach (2013)

In 2013, Target Corporation suffered a massive data breach that compromised the credit and debit card information of approximately 40 million customers. The breach occurred due to a phishing attack that targeted a third-party vendor. Once the attackers gained access, they infiltrated Target's network and extracted sensitive data.

This case study highlights the importance of securing third-party vendors and the need for comprehensive security protocols to protect against phishing attacks.

Case Study 2: The Google Docs Phishing Attack (2017)

In 2017, a sophisticated phishing attack targeted Google Docs users. Victims received emails that appeared to be from contacts, inviting them to view a document on Google Docs. The link led to a fake Google login page, which harvested user credentials. The attack spread rapidly, affecting millions of users before Google could contain it.

The Google Docs phishing attack demonstrated the dangers of highly convincing phishing emails and the importance of verifying the authenticity of unexpected emails and links.

Case Study 3: The COVID-19 Phishing Scams (2020)

The COVID-19 pandemic brought a surge in phishing scams exploiting public fear and uncertainty. Scammers sent emails and text messages claiming to provide information about COVID-19, including fake health updates, stimulus payments, and vaccination appointments. These messages often contained malicious links or attachments designed to steal personal information.

The COVID-19 phishing scams emphasized the need for heightened vigilance during times of crisis and the importance of relying on trusted sources for information.

Understanding phishing scams and how to avoid them is crucial in today's digital age. By recognizing the signs of phishing emails, adopting safe browsing habits, and utilizing security tools, you can protect yourself from these malicious attacks. Stay informed, stay vigilant, and help spread awareness to protect others from falling victim to phishing scams.

Remember, the best defense against phishing is knowledge and caution. Always think twice before clicking on links or providing personal information online. Stay safe and secure in your digital life.

Chapter 3: Tech Support Scams

In today's interconnected world, where technology permeates every aspect of our lives, the threat of tech support scams has become increasingly prevalent. These scams exploit our reliance on computers and smartphones, targeting individuals who may not be well-versed in the intricacies of technology. Fraudsters masquerade as legitimate tech support representatives, using deceitful tactics to gain access to personal information, financial data, or control over devices. Understanding and avoiding these scams is crucial for safeguarding our digital lives.

Falling victim to a tech support scam can have severe repercussions, including financial loss, identity theft, and compromised security. The stress and emotional toll of being deceived can be overwhelming. By educating ourselves about these scams, we can protect not only our personal information but also our peace of mind. This guide aims to provide a comprehensive introduction to tech support scams, offering practical advice and real-life examples to help beginners stay safe in the digital world.

Tech support scams have been around since the advent of personal computers. In the early days, these scams were relatively unsophisticated, often involving unsolicited phone calls from individuals claiming to be from well-known tech companies. They would warn the victim of a non-existent problem with their computer and offer to fix it for a fee or by gaining remote access. These early scams relied heavily on the victim's lack of technical knowledge and the novelty of home computing.

As technology advanced, so did the methods used by scammers. The advent of the internet brought a new wave of scams, including email phishing and fake websites. These scams became more complex, leveraging social engineering tactics to manipulate victims into providing sensitive information or installing malicious software. The scammers' techniques evolved to include more convincing and sophisticated approaches, such as creating fake antivirus software and exploiting vulnerabilities in popular operating systems.

In the late 2000s and early 2010s, tech support scams became more organized and widespread. Scammers began using call centers to reach a larger number of potential victims. They also started exploiting vulnerabilities in popular software and operating systems, leading to more convincing and successful scams. One significant trend in recent years is the use of pop-up messages that appear on users' screens, warning them of a supposed virus or security issue. These pop-ups often mimic legitimate alerts from antivirus software or the operating system, making them difficult to distinguish from real warnings. The user is prompted to call a toll-free number for assistance, where the scam unfolds.

With the rise of remote work and increased internet usage due to the COVID-19 pandemic, tech support scams have surged. Scammers have adapted their tactics to exploit the fears and uncertainties brought about by the pandemic, targeting individuals and businesses alike. They have taken advantage of the increased reliance on technology for work, education, and social interaction, making it even more important for everyone to be aware of these scams and how to avoid them.

Famous Tech Support Scams

Detailed descriptions of notable scams

The Microsoft Tech Support Scam

One of the most well-known scams involves fraudsters posing as Microsoft support agents. They claim that your computer is infected with malware or has critical errors that need immediate attention. These scammers often use high-pressure tactics to convince victims to grant remote access to their computers. Once access is granted, they may install malware, steal personal information, or demand payment for unnecessary services. The scammers' goal is to create a sense of urgency, making the victim believe that their computer will crash or their data will be lost if they do not act quickly.

The Apple Tech Support Scam

Similar to the Microsoft scam, this scam targets Apple users. Victims receive a call or pop-up message warning of a security issue with their Mac or iPhone. The scammers claim to be from Apple Support and guide the victim through a series of steps to "fix" the problem. These steps often involve downloading software that gives the scammer remote access to the device. Once they have access, the scammers can steal personal information or demand payment for bogus services. This scam exploits the trust that users have in the Apple brand and their reliance on Apple devices.

The IRS Tech Support Scam

Although not a tech support scam in the traditional sense, this scam involves fraudsters posing as IRS agents. They claim that the victim owes back taxes and must pay immediately to avoid arrest. The scammers often use threatening language and create a sense of fear to coerce the victim into complying. They may ask for payment via wire transfer or prepaid cards, making it difficult to trace the funds. This scam is particularly effective because it preys on people's fear of the IRS and the consequences of not paying taxes.

The Refund Scam

In this scam, the victim is contacted by someone claiming to be from a reputable company, offering a refund for a supposed overpayment or subscription cancellation. The scammer requests remote access to the victim's computer to process the refund but instead transfers money out of the victim's bank account. They may also ask for personal information, such as bank account details or social security numbers, under the guise of processing the refund. This scam often targets people who may be expecting a refund or are eager to receive money, making them more likely to comply with the scammer's requests.

Impact and consequences of these scams

The impact of tech support scams can be devastating. Victims may suffer significant financial losses, especially if they provide bank account details or credit card information. The emotional toll of being deceived can also be considerable, leading to stress, anxiety, and a loss of trust in legitimate tech support services. In some cases, scammers install ransomware or other malicious software, leading to further complications and potential data loss. The consequences of these scams can extend beyond the immediate financial impact, affecting the victim's sense of security and confidence in using technology.

How Tech Support Scams Work

Common tactics used by scammers

Scammers use a variety of tactics to trick their victims, including:

Cold calls: Unsolicited phone calls claiming to be from tech support, warning of a problem with the victim's computer. The caller often creates a sense of urgency, claiming that immediate action is needed to prevent further damage or data loss.

Pop-up warnings: Fake security alerts that appear on the victim's screen, urging them to call a support number. These pop-ups often mimic legitimate alerts from antivirus software or the operating system, making them difficult to distinguish from real warnings.

Phishing emails: Emails that appear to be from legitimate companies, prompting the victim to click on a link or download an attachment. The email may contain urgent language, claiming that the victim's account has been compromised or that immediate action is needed to prevent data loss.

Fake websites: Websites designed to look like official support pages, often reached through phishing emails or search engine manipulation. These websites may prompt the victim to enter personal information or download software that gives the scammer remote access to their computer.

Psychological tricks and technical methods

Scammers often use psychological manipulation to create a sense of urgency and fear. They may claim that the victim's computer is at immediate risk of crashing or that their personal information has been compromised. By inducing panic, scammers can persuade victims to act quickly without thinking critically. They exploit common fears and anxieties, such as the fear of losing important data or being fined by the IRS.

Technically, scammers might use remote access tools to gain control of the victim's computer. They can then install malware, change settings, or access personal files. Some scammers also use keyloggers to capture passwords and other sensitive information. These tools allow the scammer to monitor the victim's activity and gather valuable information that can be used for further fraudulent activities.

How to Avoid Tech Support Scams

Recognizing red flags and warning signs

Being aware of the common warning signs of tech support scams can help you avoid falling victim to them. Here are some red flags to watch out for:

Unsolicited contact: Legitimate tech support companies do not make unsolicited phone calls or send unsolicited emails. Be suspicious of any unexpected contact claiming to be from tech support.

Urgent warnings: Scammers often create a sense of urgency, claiming that immediate action is needed. Take a moment to think critically and verify the legitimacy of the warning.

Requests for payment: Be wary of anyone asking for payment via wire transfer, prepaid cards, or gift cards. Legitimate companies typically do not request payment through these methods.

Requests for remote access: Never grant remote access to your computer to someone you do not know and trust. If you receive a request for remote access, verify the identity of the person making the request.

Practical tips and best practices

Verify the source: If you receive a suspicious call or email, verify the source by contacting the company directly using a known, legitimate phone number or website. Do not use contact information provided in the suspicious message.

Use security software: Keep your antivirus and anti-malware software up to date to protect against threats. Regularly scan your computer for malware and other security issues.

Be cautious online: Avoid clicking on links or downloading attachments from unknown sources. Be wary of pop-up messages and do not call any phone numbers provided in them. Use caution when visiting unfamiliar websites.

Educate yourself and others: Stay informed about the latest scams and share this knowledge with friends and family. By raising awareness, you can help others avoid falling victim to scams.

Case Studies

Real-life examples and personal stories

John's Story: The Fake Microsoft Support Call

John received a call from someone claiming to be from Microsoft, warning him that his computer was infected with a virus. The caller convinced John to grant remote access to his computer. The scammer then installed malware and demanded payment to remove it. John realized it was a scam when he received a second call asking for more money. He immediately disconnected his computer from the internet and contacted his bank to report the fraud. John's experience highlights the importance of verifying unsolicited calls and being cautious about granting remote access to your computer.

Emily's Experience: The Pop-up Scam

While browsing the internet, Emily encountered a pop-up message claiming her computer was infected and she needed to call a toll-free number for support. She called the number and was persuaded to pay for unnecessary software. Emily later discovered the software was bogus and had to cancel her credit card. She reported the scam to the authorities and installed security software to protect her computer. Emily's story underscores the need to be cautious of pop-up messages and to verify the legitimacy of any support requests.

Michael's Encounter: The IRS Scam

Michael received a call from someone claiming to be from the IRS, stating that he owed back taxes and needed to pay immediately to avoid arrest. The scammer instructed Michael to purchase prepaid cards and provide the card numbers. Michael reported the incident to the real IRS, who confirmed it was a scam. He also contacted his bank to monitor his accounts for any suspicious activity. Michael's experience illustrates the importance of being skeptical of unsolicited calls demanding immediate payment and verifying the legitimacy of the caller.

Analysis of what went wrong and lessons learned

John's mistake: Granting remote access to his computer without verifying the caller's identity.

Lesson: Always verify unsolicited contacts and do not grant remote access to unknown individuals. If you receive a suspicious call, contact the company directly using a known, legitimate phone number.

Emily's mistake: Responding to a pop-up message and calling the provided number.

Lesson: Be cautious of pop-up messages and verify their legitimacy through official channels. Do not call phone numbers provided in suspicious messages.

Michael's mistake: Believing the urgent threat and complying with the scammer's demands.

Lesson: Be skeptical of unsolicited calls demanding immediate payment, especially via unusual methods. Verify the legitimacy of the caller before taking any action.

What to Do If You've Been Scammed

Immediate steps to take

Disconnect your device: If you suspect your computer has been compromised, disconnect it from the internet to prevent further access.

Scan for malware: Use trusted antivirus and anti-malware software to scan your computer and remove any malicious software. Perform a thorough scan to ensure your system is clean.

Change passwords: Change the passwords for your online accounts, especially those related to financial institutions. Use strong, unique passwords for each account.

Report the scam: Contact your bank or credit card company to report any fraudulent charges. Also, report the scam to relevant authorities, such as the Federal Trade Commission (FTC) or your country's equivalent. Reporting the scam can help prevent others from falling victim to the same scheme.

Official tech support: Contact the legitimate support team of your device or software manufacturer for assistance. They can help you secure your device and recover from the scam.

Consumer protection agencies: Reach out to consumer protection agencies for guidance and to report the scam. These agencies can provide resources and support for scam victims.

Online resources: Use online resources and forums to learn more about recent scams and how to protect yourself. Many websites offer tips and advice on avoiding scams and staying safe online.

Recap of key points

Tech support scams are a prevalent and evolving threat in today's digital world. By understanding how these scams work, recognizing the warning signs, and knowing how to respond, you can protect yourself and others from becoming victims. Education and vigilance are your best defenses against these malicious schemes. Remember to verify unsolicited contacts, use security software, and be cautious online.

Encouragement to stay vigilant and informed

Stay informed about the latest scams and share your knowledge with friends and family. By staying vigilant and proactive, you can help create a safer online environment for everyone. Remember, if something seems suspicious, it's always better to verify before taking action. Protecting yourself from tech support scams requires continuous awareness and education. By doing so, you can enjoy the benefits of technology without falling prey to fraudsters.

Chapter 4: Online Dating Scams

The history of online dating scams is as old as online dating itself. In the late 1990s and early 2000s, as the internet became more accessible, online dating platforms like Match.com and eHarmony emerged, offering new ways for people to find love. Initially, these platforms were met with excitement and trust. People were thrilled with the novel concept of finding a partner online, leading to an explosion in the popularity of these sites.

However, it didn't take long for scammers to exploit this new avenue. The early scams were relatively simple. Scammers would create fake profiles, establish a connection with their targets, and then fabricate a sob story to elicit money. These early frauds often involved basic stories about sudden financial crises, such as a broken-down car or an urgent medical bill. Despite their simplicity, these scams were effective because online daters, eager to find love, were often willing to overlook red flags.

As online dating grew in popularity, so did the sophistication of these scams. Today, online dating scams are a global issue, with scammers using advanced tactics and technologies to deceive their victims. Current trends in online dating scams include the use of artificial intelligence to create convincing fake profiles and deepfake technology to create realistic videos and images. According to the Federal Trade Commission (FTC), losses due to romance scams in the United States alone exceeded $300 million in 2020, highlighting the significant impact these scams have on society.

Famous Online Dating Scams

The Nigerian Prince Scam

One of the earliest and most infamous online scams is the Nigerian Prince scam. Although it predates online dating, this scam has found its way into the dating world. Scammers, posing as royalty or wealthy individuals, promise their targets a significant sum of money in exchange for a small upfront payment. The scammer's narrative often involves needing help to transfer a large inheritance out of their country. Despite its outlandish premise, the Nigerian Prince scam continues to ensnare victims, causing significant financial losses.

Catfishing

Catfishing involves creating a fictitious online persona to deceive others. Famous cases, like the one involving Notre Dame football star Manti Te'o, who was duped into believing he was in a relationship with a non-existent woman, have brought significant attention to this type of scam. Catfishing can lead to severe emotional trauma for victims, who often invest considerable time and emotional energy into these fake relationships. The psychological manipulation involved in catfishing is profound, often leaving victims feeling humiliated and betrayed.

Romance scams are among the most common and damaging online dating scams. Scammers create fake profiles on dating sites and apps, often using stolen photos of attractive individuals to lure their targets. Once they have gained their victim's trust, they fabricate a crisis that requires financial assistance. Notable cases include victims losing their life savings or falling into severe debt. The psychological manipulation involved in these scams can be as damaging as the financial losses. Scammers often invest months in building a relationship before making any requests for money, making it harder for victims to recognize the deceit.

The Military Romance Scam

In this scam, fraudsters impersonate military personnel, exploiting the trust and respect that soldiers typically command. They often claim to be stationed in remote locations and unable to access their funds, asking their victims to send money for various fabricated needs. Real-life examples of this scam include individuals being duped out of thousands of dollars, believing they were helping a soldier in need. This scam is particularly insidious because it preys on the noble intentions of those who wish to support their country's servicemen and women.

To avoid falling victim to online dating scams, it's crucial to recognize the red flags. Common warning signs include profiles that seem too good to be true, rapid declarations of love, and requests for money. Scammers often use flattery and create a sense of urgency to manipulate their targets. They may claim to have fallen in love very quickly or have a crisis that requires immediate financial assistance.

Never share personal information such as your home address, financial details, or social security number with someone you've just met online. Scammers can use this information for identity theft or further manipulation. Be cautious about the information you share publicly on your dating profile as well, as scammers can use this to tailor their approach.

Verify the identity of the person you are communicating with. Use video calls to ensure the person matches their profile pictures. Be wary of individuals who avoid face-to-face communication or have inconsistent stories. If someone is reluctant to meet in person or keeps making excuses, it could be a sign that they are not who they claim to be.

Leverage technology to protect yourself. Many dating platforms offer verification services and tools to report suspicious profiles. Additionally, there are apps and websites dedicated to exposing and tracking scammers. Use these tools to your advantage to stay safe. Websites like ScamHaters United and services like Google Image Search can help verify if the photos used in profiles are genuine.

If you suspect you've encountered a scammer, report it to the dating platform and seek professional help. Organizations like the FTC, the Internet Crime Complaint Center (IC3), and non-profits offer resources and support for scam victims. Legal avenues may also be available to help recover lost funds. Consulting with a lawyer or a financial advisor can also provide you with the necessary steps to take if you've been scammed.

Case Study 1: The Tale of Jane Doe

Jane Doe, a successful businesswoman, met a charming man named Alex on a popular dating site. Alex claimed to be a wealthy entrepreneur working on an overseas project. After months of daily communication and building a deep emotional connection, Alex informed Jane of a financial crisis affecting his project. Trusting him, Jane sent him $50,000. Eventually, Alex disappeared, and Jane discovered that his entire persona was fabricated. This case highlights the importance of verifying identities and being cautious of financial requests. Jane's story serves as a cautionary tale about the importance of skepticism and due diligence.

Case Study 2: John Smith's Experience

John Smith, a retired military veteran, was approached by someone claiming to be a female soldier stationed abroad. She shared stories of her service and personal struggles, eventually asking John for money to return home. Moved by her plight, John sent her several thousand dollars. When the requests for money kept coming, John grew suspicious and contacted military support services, discovering the scam. This experience underscores the need for skepticism and the importance of seeking external validation. John's experience illustrates the vulnerability even seasoned individuals can face when dealing with sophisticated scammers.

Case Study 3: A Community's Response

A small town in the Midwest experienced a surge in online dating scams, affecting many residents. The community came together to raise awareness, hosting workshops and support groups for victims. Local law enforcement collaborated with national agencies to investigate and prevent further scams. This collective effort not only helped victims recover but also educated others on recognizing and avoiding scams. The community's response serves as a powerful example of the impact of collective action and support. Through their efforts, they managed to significantly reduce the incidence of scams and support those who had been affected.

Online dating scams are a pervasive and evolving threat in the digital age. By understanding their history, recognizing famous scams, and learning how to avoid them, individuals can protect themselves from becoming victims. The real-life case studies illustrate the profound impact these scams can have on people's lives. Staying informed, vigilant, and cautious is the best defense against online dating scams. Remember, the quest for love should never come at the cost of your safety and well-being.

This chapter aims to provide a comprehensive guide for beginners to navigate the world of online dating safely. By shedding light on the tactics used by scammers and offering practical advice, it empowers readers to protect themselves and others from falling prey to these malicious schemes. Awareness and education are the first steps in safeguarding your heart and finances in the world of online dating.

Chapter 5: The IRS impersonation scam

IRS impersonation scams have become increasingly prevalent in recent years, causing significant financial and emotional distress for countless individuals. These scams are sophisticated schemes designed to deceive taxpayers into believing they owe money to the IRS, often leading to the loss of hard-earned savings. The importance of understanding and recognizing these scams cannot be overstated.

This chapter aims to provide a comprehensive guide to IRS impersonation scams, offering insight into their history, the tactics employed by scammers, and practical advice on how to avoid falling victim to such schemes. By raising awareness and educating the public, we can collectively reduce the impact of these scams and protect our communities.

In the following, we will explore the evolution of IRS impersonation scams, delve into some of the most infamous cases, dissect the anatomy of a typical scam, and provide actionable steps to safeguard against them. Additionally, we will examine real-life case studies that highlight the devastating effects of these scams and the resilience of those who have been targeted.

Whether you are a taxpayer looking to protect yourself or someone interested in understanding the mechanisms of modern scams, this book will serve as a valuable resource. Let's embark on this journey to uncover the dark world of IRS impersonation scams and arm ourselves with the knowledge needed to stay safe.

IRS impersonation scams have a long and troubling history, dating back to the early days of the Internal Revenue Service itself. As long as there have been taxes, there have been individuals attempting to exploit the system and prey on unsuspecting taxpayers. Understanding the history of these scams provides crucial context for the sophisticated tactics used by scammers today.

The earliest recorded IRS scams were relatively simple, relying on the limited communication methods available at the time. In the late 19th and early 20th centuries, con artists would send fraudulent letters to taxpayers, claiming to represent the IRS and demanding immediate payment for back taxes. These letters often contained official-looking seals and intimidating language, designed to coerce compliance through fear.

As communication technology advanced, so did the methods employed by scammers. The introduction of the telephone provided a new avenue for fraudsters to directly contact potential victims. Throughout the mid-20th century, phone scams became increasingly common, with criminals posing as IRS agents and using aggressive tactics to demand payment.

One of the significant milestones in the history of IRS impersonation scams occurred in the 1970s with the rise of telemarketing fraud. Scammers began to use sophisticated scripts and psychological manipulation to extract money from victims. These early scams laid the groundwork for the more elaborate schemes that would emerge in the digital age.

The advent of the internet in the late 20th century brought about a seismic shift in the landscape of IRS impersonation scams. Email and online communication allowed scammers to reach a broader audience with minimal effort. Phishing emails, designed to look like official IRS correspondence, became a common tool for criminals. These emails often included malicious links or attachments that, when clicked, would steal personal information or install harmful software on the victim's computer.

In the 21st century, the evolution of technology has further transformed IRS impersonation scams. Scammers now employ a variety of sophisticated techniques, including spoofing caller ID information to make it appear as though calls are coming from the IRS. They use robocalls to reach thousands of potential victims simultaneously, increasing their chances of success.

Additionally, the rise of social media has provided scammers with new opportunities to gather information about their targets. By piecing together details from social media profiles, criminals can create convincing narratives that make their scams more believable.

Another technological advancement that has impacted IRS impersonation scams is the use of cryptocurrency. Scammers often demand payment in cryptocurrencies like Bitcoin, which are difficult to trace and can be transferred quickly. This has made it harder for law enforcement to track and recover stolen funds.

The history of IRS impersonation scams is a testament to the ingenuity and persistence of scammers. By understanding how these scams have evolved over time, we can better equip ourselves to recognize and combat them in the present day.

IRS impersonation scams have garnered significant media attention over the years, particularly when large-scale operations have been uncovered or high-profile individuals have been targeted. Understanding these famous scams provides insight into the methods used by scammers and highlights the importance of vigilance.

One of the most infamous IRS impersonation scams originated from call centers in India. In 2016, U.S. authorities uncovered a massive operation involving hundreds of employees working in call centers who posed as IRS agents. These scammers would call American taxpayers, using threats of arrest, deportation, or license revocation to coerce them into making immediate payments via prepaid debit cards or wire transfers.

The scale of this operation was staggering. It's estimated that over 15,000 victims were scammed out of more than $300 million. The scam was highly organized, with scripts and training programs designed to teach employees how to manipulate victims effectively. The bust of this operation was a significant victory for law enforcement, but it also highlighted the global nature of modern scams and the challenges of combating them.

The Case of Steven Martinez

Steven Martinez, a former IRS revenue agent, used his insider knowledge to perpetrate a different kind of IRS scam. Martinez, who worked in the IRS's San Diego office, stole $11 million from clients by promising to resolve their tax debts and then siphoning the money for his personal use. His position within the IRS lent him an air of legitimacy that made it easier to deceive his victims.

Martinez's case is a stark reminder that scams can sometimes come from individuals within the system. He was eventually caught and sentenced to 24 years in prison, but not before causing significant financial harm to his clients. His story underscores the importance of due diligence, even when dealing with seemingly trustworthy individuals.

The TurboTax Phishing Scams

TurboTax, a popular tax preparation software, has been used as a cover for numerous phishing scams. In these scams, criminals send emails that appear to be from TurboTax, urging recipients to update their accounts or verify their information. The emails contain links to fake websites that look nearly identical to the official TurboTax site, where victims are prompted to enter sensitive information.

These phishing scams are particularly effective because they target individuals who are already in the process of dealing with their taxes and might not think twice about an email from a service they use. Once the scammers have the victims' personal and financial information, they can file fraudulent tax returns and steal refunds. TurboTax has taken steps to combat these scams, including providing educational resources and implementing more robust security measures.

The John Reinke Scam

John Reinke was a financial advisor who orchestrated a complex tax scam that bilked clients out of millions of dollars. Posing as an IRS agent, Reinke convinced his clients that they owed substantial amounts in back taxes and that he could help them negotiate settlements. In reality, he was funneling their payments into his own accounts.

Reinke's scam was notable for its sophistication and the trust he was able to build with his victims. He used his position as a financial advisor to gain access to his clients' financial information and then exploited that trust to deceive them. His eventual arrest and conviction were the result of a joint effort by the IRS and the FBI, highlighting the importance of inter-agency cooperation in combating complex scams.

These high-profile scams have had a significant impact on the victims involved, often resulting in substantial financial losses and emotional distress. The public awareness generated by media coverage of these scams has been a double-edged sword. On one hand, it has increased awareness and prompted more people to be cautious when dealing with unsolicited communications from supposed IRS agents. On the other hand, the persistence and adaptability of scammers mean that new victims are continuously being targeted.

These famous cases serve as cautionary tales and emphasize the importance of staying informed about the latest scam tactics. By learning from the experiences of those who have been scammed, we can better protect ourselves and our loved ones from falling victim to similar schemes.

Understanding the structure and tactics of IRS impersonation scams is crucial in recognizing and avoiding them. This chapter breaks down the common elements of these scams, highlighting the psychological manipulation and communication methods used by scammers.

Common Tactics Used by Scammers

Impersonation of IRS Officials

Scammers often pose as IRS agents, using fake badge numbers and official-sounding titles to lend credibility to their claims.

They may provide personal information about the victim (obtained through prior research or data breaches) to appear more legitimate.

Urgent and Threatening Language

The core tactic is to create a sense of urgency. Scammers use threats of arrest, deportation, or legal action to pressure victims into immediate compliance.

They may claim that there is a limited time to resolve the issue to prevent legal consequences, pushing victims to act quickly without verification.

Payment Demands

Scammers typically demand payment through unconventional means such as prepaid debit cards, wire transfers, or, increasingly, cryptocurrencies.

They instruct victims to purchase specific types of payment methods and provide instructions on how to transfer the funds.

Spoofing Technology

Caller ID spoofing is a common technique, making it appear as if the call is coming from the IRS or another government agency.

Email spoofing and phishing websites are used to mimic official IRS communications and websites.

Psychological Manipulation Techniques

Fear and Intimidation

Scammers exploit the natural fear of legal trouble and authority figures. The threat of jail time, fines, or deportation creates a panic response.

Victims are often too scared to think rationally and comply quickly to avoid the threatened consequences.

Authority

By posing as IRS agents or officials, scammers leverage the inherent authority and trust associated with the IRS.

The use of official titles, jargon, and formal communication styles reinforces the perception of legitimacy.

Isolation

Scammers often instruct victims not to tell anyone about the situation or seek advice, isolating them from potential support and verification.

This isolation tactic prevents victims from consulting with family members, friends, or financial advisors who might recognize the scam.

Communication Methods

Phone Calls

The most common method involves phone calls from scammers posing as IRS agents. These calls may be live or automated robocalls.

Scammers use aggressive tactics, often calling multiple times to increase pressure.

Emails

Phishing emails are crafted to look like official IRS communications. They may contain logos, formal language, and links to fraudulent websites.

These emails often request personal information, such as Social Security numbers or bank account details.

Letters

Some scams involve physical letters sent through the mail, designed to look like official IRS correspondence.

These letters may use official-looking letterheads and seals to deceive recipients.

By dissecting the anatomy of IRS impersonation scams, we can better understand how scammers operate and the tactics they use to deceive their victims. Awareness of these common elements is the first step in recognizing and avoiding these scams.

Avoiding IRS impersonation scams requires vigilance and knowledge. This chapter provides practical advice on recognizing red flags, verifying IRS communications, protecting personal information, and taking action if you suspect a scam.

Recognizing Red Flags

Unsolicited Communication

The IRS will not initiate contact with taxpayers by phone, email, or social media to request personal or financial information.

Be wary of any unexpected communication claiming to be from the IRS, especially if it demands immediate action or payment.

Threatening Language

The IRS does not use aggressive or threatening language. Legitimate IRS communication will not threaten arrest, deportation, or license revocation.

Any message that uses such threats is a clear red flag.

Unusual Payment Methods

The IRS will not ask for payment via prepaid debit cards, wire transfers, or cryptocurrency.

Requests for these types of payment should be treated with suspicion.

Verifying IRS Communication

Check Official Channels

If you receive a suspicious call or email, do not provide any information or make any payments. Instead, contact the IRS directly using the contact information on their official website.

Verify any communication by calling the IRS at their official phone number (1-800-829-1040) or visiting an IRS office.

Look for Official IRS Letters

The IRS typically communicates by mail. Legitimate letters will have official IRS letterheads and detailed information about your tax situation.

Compare any suspicious letter with previous IRS correspondence to check for consistency.

Best Practices for Protecting Personal Information

Safeguard Personal Information

Do not share your Social Security number, bank account information, or other sensitive details unless you are certain of the recipient's legitimacy.

Be cautious when sharing personal information over the phone or online, especially with unsolicited contacts.

Use Strong, Unique Passwords

Protect your online accounts with strong, unique passwords. Use a combination of letters, numbers, and special characters.

Consider using a password manager to keep track of your passwords securely.

Monitor Your Financial Accounts

Regularly check your bank and credit card statements for any unauthorized transactions.

Set up alerts for your financial accounts to notify you of any suspicious activity.

Steps to Take if You Suspect a Scam

Do Not Engage

If you suspect a scam, do not engage with the caller or email sender. Hang up the phone or delete the email without responding.

Avoid clicking on any links or downloading attachments from suspicious emails.

Report the Scam

Report IRS impersonation scams to the Treasury Inspector General for Tax Administration (TIGTA) online at www.treasury.gov/tigta or by calling 1-800-366-4484.

Report phishing emails to the IRS at phishing@irs.gov.

Seek Assistance

If you have provided personal information or made a payment to a scammer, contact your financial institutions immediately to secure your accounts.

Consider placing a fraud alert or credit freeze on your credit reports to prevent further damage.

By following these guidelines, you can significantly reduce your risk of falling victim to an IRS impersonation scam. Staying informed and cautious is key to protecting yourself and your financial well-being.

Understanding real-life case studies of IRS impersonation scams helps illustrate the tactics scammers use and the impact these scams have on victims. This chapter delves into several notable cases, exploring the methods used, the consequences for victims, and the law enforcement response.

Case Study 1: The Elderly Victim

Background:

Jane Doe, an 82-year-old widow, received a call from someone claiming to be an IRS agent. The caller ID showed a Washington, D.C. area code, adding legitimacy to the call. The "agent" informed Jane that she owed $5,000 in back taxes and threatened her with immediate arrest if she did not pay.

Scam Tactics:

Intimidation and Urgency: The scammer used a stern tone and threatened Jane with arrest and asset seizure.

Payment via Prepaid Cards: Jane was instructed to purchase prepaid debit cards and provide the card numbers over the phone.

Isolation: The scammer told Jane not to inform anyone, claiming it was a confidential matter to avoid further legal complications.

Impact:

Jane, frightened and confused, complied with the scammer's demands, losing $5,000 of her savings. The emotional toll was significant, leading to anxiety and mistrust of future communications from legitimate authorities.

Law Enforcement Response:

Jane reported the incident to the local police, who then involved federal authorities. Unfortunately, the scammer could not be traced, but the case was used in public awareness campaigns to educate others.

Lesson Learned:

This case highlights the importance of recognizing red flags, such as urgent demands for payment via unconventional methods, and the need for public education, especially among vulnerable populations like the elderly.

Case Study 2: The Small Business Owner

Background:

John Smith, a small business owner, received an email that appeared to be from the IRS, notifying him of a supposed audit. The email contained a link to a website where John was instructed to enter his personal and business financial information.

Scam Tactics:

Phishing Email: The email was professionally crafted, complete with IRS logos and formal language.

Fake Website: The link led to a fake IRS website that collected John's sensitive information.

Follow-Up Calls: After John entered his details, he received follow-up calls from scammers posing as IRS agents to further validate the scam.

Impact:

John unknowingly provided his Social Security number, business EIN, and bank account details. The scammers used this information to steal his identity and file fraudulent tax returns. John faced a lengthy process of clearing his name and restoring his financial accounts.

Law Enforcement Response:

The incident was reported to the IRS and the Federal Trade Commission (FTC). While the scammers were not apprehended, the authorities provided John with resources to protect his identity and prevent further fraud.

Lesson Learned:

This case underscores the need for skepticism regarding unsolicited emails and the importance of verifying the legitimacy of any communication claiming to be from the IRS. Businesses, in particular, should implement strict protocols for handling sensitive information.

Case Study 3: The Tech-Savvy Teen

Background:

Emily, a 19-year-old college student, received a call from someone claiming to be an IRS agent. The caller threatened her with arrest for tax evasion if she did not pay a supposed overdue tax bill. Despite her tech-savvy nature, Emily was caught off guard by the threatening tone.

Scam Tactics:

Caller ID Spoofing: The call appeared to come from the IRS.

Immediate Payment Demand: Emily was instructed to wire money through a transfer service.

Emotional Manipulation: The scammer played on Emily's fear of legal trouble and her inexperience with tax matters.

Impact:

Emily transferred $1,500 before realizing she had been scammed. The financial loss was significant for a college student, and she felt embarrassed and betrayed by the experience.

Law Enforcement Response:

Emily reported the scam to campus security and local law enforcement, who guided her in contacting the IRS and TIGTA.

Awareness programs were subsequently conducted on campus to educate students about such scams.

Lesson Learned:

This case illustrates that even tech-savvy individuals can fall victim to well-crafted scams. It highlights the importance of public awareness and education campaigns, especially targeting young adults who may be unfamiliar with tax procedures.

Case Study 4: The Veteran

Background:

Tom, a retired military veteran, received a letter in the mail claiming to be from the IRS, stating that he owed $8,000 in back taxes. The letter looked official, complete with an IRS letterhead and seal.

Scam Tactics:

Official-Looking Correspondence: The letter was designed to mimic genuine IRS communication.

Payment Instructions: Tom was instructed to call a number to arrange payment.

Personalized Information: The letter included personal details, likely obtained from previous data breaches, to add credibility.

Impact:

Tom was skeptical but called the number out of concern. The scammer on the other end demanded immediate payment via a wire transfer. Tom lost $8,000, a significant portion of his savings.

Law Enforcement Response:

Tom reported the incident to the IRS and local law enforcement. Although the funds were not recovered, the case was used to help develop better protective measures and public awareness efforts.

Lesson Learned:

This case demonstrates that scammers are becoming increasingly sophisticated in their tactics. It reinforces the importance of verifying any IRS correspondence through official channels before taking any action.

The case studies presented in this chapter offer a sobering look at the diverse methods used by scammers and the profound effects these scams have on victims. They also provide valuable lessons on the importance of skepticism, verification, and awareness in protecting oneself from IRS impersonation scams.

IRS impersonation scams are a pervasive threat that can affect anyone, regardless of age, background, or financial status. By understanding the history of these scams, recognizing the tactics used by scammers, and learning from real-life case studies, we can better protect ourselves and our communities.

Key takeaways from this chapter include:

Always verify any communication claiming to be from the IRS through official channels.

Be aware of common red flags, such as unsolicited contact, urgent threats, and demands for unconventional payment methods.

Protect your personal information and be cautious when sharing sensitive details.

If you suspect a scam, report it immediately to the appropriate authorities and seek assistance to mitigate any potential damage.

Staying informed and vigilant is the best defense against IRS impersonation scams. By sharing this knowledge with others, we can collectively reduce the impact of these fraudulent schemes and safeguard our financial well-being.

Chapter 6: The Fake Job Scam

Fake job scams are not a new phenomenon. They have been around for centuries, evolving with changes in society and technology. In the early days, scammers would place ads in newspapers, promising high-paying jobs to lure in unsuspecting individuals. As technology advanced, so did the scams. The rise of the internet brought about a new era of job scams, with fraudulent job offers being sent via email and posted on job search websites.

One of the earliest recorded job scams involved con artists who promised lucrative positions in far-off lands. They would collect fees from job seekers for travel expenses and paperwork, only to disappear once they had the money. These scams exploited the desperation of people looking for better opportunities, a tactic that remains effective today.

With the advent of the internet, job scams became more sophisticated and widespread. Scammers could reach a larger audience with less effort, making it easier to deceive job seekers. The anonymity of the internet also provided a shield for scammers, making it difficult for authorities to track them down.

Social media has further complicated the landscape of job scams. Scammers now use platforms like LinkedIn and Facebook to create fake profiles and job postings, making their scams appear more legitimate. They can also use these platforms to gather information about potential victims, increasing their chances of success.

Over the years, several fake job scams have gained notoriety for their scale and impact. These scams not only highlight the creativity of scammers but also serve as cautionary tales for job seekers.

One of the most famous scams is the Nigerian Prince job offer. In this scam, individuals receive an email from someone claiming to be a Nigerian prince or government official who needs help transferring a large sum of money. In return for their assistance, the job seeker is promised a generous reward. However, they are first asked to pay various fees to facilitate the transfer, and once they do, the scammer disappears.

The Fake Job Agency Scams

Fake job agencies are another common scam. These agencies claim to have exclusive access to high-paying job opportunities. They charge job seekers a fee for their services, promising to secure them a job. However, once the fee is paid, the agency provides either no job leads or bogus ones, leaving the job seeker out of pocket and without a job.

Online job boards and classified sites are rife with fake job postings. These scams often involve positions that offer unusually high salaries for minimal work. Job seekers are asked to provide personal information or pay upfront fees for background checks, training, or equipment. Once the scammer has what they want, they vanish, leaving the job seeker vulnerable to identity theft or financial loss.

Identifying fake job scams can be challenging, especially when they are cleverly disguised as legitimate opportunities. However, there are several red flags that job seekers can watch out for.

Unusual Job Requirements and High Salaries for Entry-Level Positions

One common characteristic of fake job scams is the promise of high salaries for jobs that require little to no experience. If a job offer seems too good to be true, it probably is. Be wary of positions that offer substantial pay for minimal effort, as these are often traps set by scammers.

Legitimate employers do not ask for sensitive personal information (such as Social Security numbers or bank account details) or payments upfront. If a job offer requires you to provide such information or pay for anything before you start working, it is likely a scam.

Scammers often use poorly written job postings and emails. Look out for spelling and grammatical errors, vague job descriptions, and unprofessional language. While some legitimate job postings may contain minor errors, a combination of these issues should raise a red flag.

Legitimate job postings typically include detailed information about the company, including its name, address, and contact details. If a job posting lacks this information or if the company cannot be easily found online, it may be a scam.

Avoiding fake job scams requires vigilance and due diligence. By following these practical tips, job seekers can protect themselves from falling victim to scams.

Before applying for a job, take the time to research the company. Check their official website and look for reviews from current and former employees. Verify that the job posting is listed on the company's official site. If you cannot find any credible information about the company, proceed with caution.

Utilize reputable job search platforms that have measures in place to detect and prevent fake job postings. Sites like LinkedIn, Indeed, and Glassdoor offer safer environments for job seekers. However, remain cautious even on these platforms, as scammers can still slip through the cracks.

Never share sensitive personal information with a potential employer until you are certain the job offer is legitimate. Legitimate employers will not ask for your Social Security number, bank account details, or other sensitive information during the initial stages of the hiring process.

If you receive a job offer that seems suspicious, consult trusted sources such as family, friends, or career advisors. They may be able to provide insights or spot red flags that you missed. Additionally, you can report suspicious job offers to authorities or organizations that specialize in dealing with job scams.

Learning from real-life experiences can provide valuable insights into how job scams operate and how to avoid them. Here are a few case studies of individuals who encountered fake job scams.

Victim Case Studies

Case Study 1: The Too-Good-to-Be-True Offer

Maria received an email offering her a high-paying data entry job that required no experience. The job promised a salary much higher than industry standards. Excited by the prospect, Maria provided her personal information and paid a fee for a "background check." She later discovered that the job did not exist, and her information was used for identity theft.

Case Study 2: The Fake Job Agency

John was approached by a job agency that claimed to have exclusive access to top companies. He paid a substantial fee for their services but received no job leads in return. Further investigation revealed that the agency was a front for a scam operation.

Success Stories of Avoiding Scams

Case Study 3: Researching and Verifying

Sarah received a job offer from a company she had never heard of. Instead of immediately accepting, she researched the company online, checked their official website, and contacted them directly to verify the offer. Her diligence revealed that the job offer was fake, and she avoided becoming a victim.

Case Study 4: Consulting Trusted Sources

When Mark received a job offer that seemed too good to be true, he consulted his career advisor. The advisor noticed several red flags and advised Mark to decline the offer. This saved Mark from falling into a scam.

These case studies highlight the importance of vigilance, research, and consulting trusted sources when evaluating job offers. They demonstrate that while scammers are crafty, taking proactive steps can significantly reduce the risk of falling victim to their schemes.

Fake job scams are a pervasive and evolving threat to job seekers. By understanding the history and tactics of these scams, recognizing red flags, and taking precautionary measures, you can protect yourself from falling victim. Remember to stay informed, be cautious, and share your knowledge with others. Together, we can create a safer job market for everyone.

Additional Resources

For further information and assistance in avoiding fake job scams, consider the following resources:

Federal Trade Commission (FTC) – Job Scams

Better Business Bureau (BBB) – Employment Scams

The Balance Careers – How to Avoid Job Scams

Scamwatch – Job and Employment Scams

Chapter 7: Identity Theft Scams

Identity theft is one of the fastest-growing crimes in the world today. It occurs when someone unlawfully obtains and uses another person's personal information, typically for financial gain. This can include stealing social security numbers, credit card information, bank account details, or even medical records. The consequences of identity theft can be devastating, leading to financial loss, damaged credit, and emotional distress.

Importance of Understanding Identity Theft Scams

With the increasing reliance on digital technology and the internet, identity theft has become more prevalent and sophisticated. Scammers are constantly devising new methods to trick individuals into revealing their personal information. Understanding how these scams work and how to protect oneself is crucial for safeguarding personal information and preventing financial and emotional harm.

This chapter aims to provide readers with a comprehensive understanding of identity theft scams, including their history, famous cases, and practical advice on prevention and recovery. Written in a conversational tone, it is designed to be accessible to beginners who may not be familiar with the complexities of identity theft. By the end of this book, you will have the knowledge and tools to protect yourself from becoming a victim of identity theft.

Identity theft is the act of stealing someone's personal information without their permission, often for the purpose of committing fraud or theft. This can involve a wide range of activities, from unauthorized credit card transactions to complex schemes involving multiple victims and perpetrators. The stolen information can be used to open new accounts, make purchases, or even commit crimes in the victim's name.

Types of Identity Theft

Financial Identity Theft: Using someone's identity to access their bank accounts, credit cards, or take out loans. This is the most common type of identity theft and can result in significant financial loss.

Medical Identity Theft: Stealing personal information to obtain medical services or drugs. This can lead to incorrect medical records and denied insurance claims.

Criminal Identity Theft: Using another person's identity when arrested or charged with a crime. This can result in a criminal record for the victim and significant legal troubles.

Synthetic Identity Theft: Combining real and fake information to create a new, false identity. This type of theft is often used to open new accounts and make fraudulent purchases.

Statistics and Impact on Individuals and Society

Identity theft affects millions of people annually, resulting in billions of dollars in financial losses. Victims often face long-term consequences, such as damaged credit scores, legal complications, and significant emotional stress. The ripple effect can also impact businesses and institutions, leading to increased costs and compromised trust. According to the Federal Trade Commission (FTC), there were over 4 million reports of identity theft and fraud in 2020 alone.

Before the digital age, identity theft was primarily a physical crime. Thieves would steal wallets, rummage through trash for discarded bank statements, or intercept mail. These methods, while rudimentary, could still lead to significant financial damage. In the early 20th century, criminals would create fake identities using forged documents to commit fraud.

The advent of the internet and digital technologies revolutionized identity theft. Email scams, online shopping, and social media introduced new avenues for criminals to exploit. Phishing scams became a common method for tricking individuals into revealing personal information. As more people started shopping and banking online, identity thieves found new opportunities to steal sensitive information.

1990s: The rise of the internet brought about the first major wave of online identity theft. Hackers would use techniques like phishing and malware to steal personal information.

2000s: Data breaches at large companies exposed millions of consumers to potential fraud. High-profile breaches at companies like TJX and Heartland Payment Systems highlighted the vulnerabilities in data security.

2010s: Social media and mobile devices introduced new vulnerabilities. Identity thieves began exploiting social media profiles to gather information about potential victims.

2020s: Advanced hacking techniques and the use of AI have made identity theft even more sophisticated. Cybercriminals now use AI to create convincing phishing scams and deepfakes to manipulate audio and video.

Identity theft scams have varied widely in their methods and scope. Some of the most infamous scams have had far-reaching impacts, affecting millions of people and costing billions of dollars.

Understanding these scams can provide valuable lessons in how to protect oneself from similar threats.

The ChoicePoint Scandal: In 2005, data aggregator ChoicePoint suffered a breach that exposed the personal information of over 163,000 individuals. The company was fined heavily and had to implement significant changes to its data security practices. The breach occurred when identity thieves posed as legitimate businesses to gain access to ChoicePoint's database.

The Equifax Data Breach: In 2017, credit reporting agency Equifax announced a data breach that affected 147 million people. Hackers accessed names, social security numbers, birth dates, addresses, and in some cases, driver's license numbers. The breach highlighted the vulnerabilities in data security and the importance of protecting personal information.

The IRS Tax Refund Scam: Criminals file fraudulent tax returns using stolen personal information to claim refunds. This scam has resulted in billions of dollars in losses and a massive backlog of fraudulent cases for the IRS to address. Victims often find out about the scam when their legitimate tax return is rejected because a return has already been filed in their name.

Keep personal information secure: Shred documents containing personal information before discarding them. Use secure passwords and change them regularly. Avoid sharing personal information over the phone, email, or social media unless you are sure of the recipient's identity.

Monitor financial accounts: Regularly check bank and credit card statements for unauthorized transactions. Set up alerts to notify you of any suspicious activity.

Be cautious with sharing information: Avoid sharing personal information over the phone, email, or social media unless you are sure of the recipient's identity. Be mindful of what you share online and adjust your privacy settings accordingly.

Use strong, unique passwords: Combine letters, numbers, and symbols, and avoid using easily guessable information like birthdays. Consider using a password manager to keep track of your passwords.

Enable two-factor authentication: This adds an extra layer of security by requiring a second form of identification, such as a code sent to your phone.

Be wary of public Wi-Fi: Avoid accessing sensitive information over public networks, which can be easily compromised. Use a virtual private network (VPN) to secure your internet connection.

Email and text scams: Look out for unsolicited messages asking for personal information. Verify the sender's identity before responding. Be cautious of links and attachments in emails from unknown senders.

Phone scams: Be cautious of callers claiming to be from legitimate organizations and asking for personal details. Hang up and call the organization directly using a known phone number to verify the caller's identity.

Social media scams: Be mindful of friend requests and messages from unknown individuals. Avoid clicking on links or downloading files from unknown sources.

Secure your mail: Use a locked mailbox and consider opting for electronic statements to reduce the risk of mail theft. Be cautious of unsolicited mail asking for personal information.

Be cautious with documents: Keep important documents in a safe place and only carry what you need. Shred documents containing personal information before discarding them.

Detailed Real-Life Stories of Identity Theft Victims

Case Study 1: A Financial Fraud Victim

Jane, a teacher from California, discovered that her credit card had been used to make several large purchases she didn't recognize. After contacting her bank, she learned that her identity had been stolen and used to open new accounts in her name. The process of clearing her name took over a year and involved numerous legal battles and credit report disputes. Jane's experience highlights the importance of regularly monitoring your financial accounts and promptly reporting any suspicious activity.

Case Study 2: Medical Identity Theft

John, a construction worker, found himself denied medical treatment because his insurance benefits had been maxed out. Investigations revealed that his personal information had been used by someone else to receive extensive medical services. This not only affected his insurance but also left him with inaccurate medical records. John's case underscores the need to monitor your medical records and be cautious of sharing your personal information with healthcare providers.

Case Study 3: Social Security Fraud

Emily, a retiree, received a notice from the IRS about unreported income. She discovered that her social security number had been used to file false tax returns and claim refunds. Clearing up the fraud involved working with multiple government agencies and took several years. Emily's story highlights the importance of securing your social security number and being vigilant about monitoring your tax records.

Each of these cases highlights different aspects of identity theft and the importance of vigilance. Common preventive measures include monitoring credit reports, securing personal information, and promptly addressing any suspicious activity. By staying informed and proactive, you can reduce the risk of becoming a victim of identity theft.

Immediate Steps to Take

Contact financial institutions: Notify your bank and credit card companies of any fraudulent activity. They can freeze your accounts and help you dispute any unauthorized transactions.

Place a fraud alert: Contact one of the major credit bureaus (Equifax, Experian, or TransUnion) to place a fraud alert on your credit report. This will notify creditors to take extra steps to verify your identity before opening new accounts.

File a report: Report the theft to the Federal Trade Commission (FTC) and your local police department. The FTC's Identity Theft Report can help you create a recovery plan and provide proof to businesses and law enforcement.

FTC Identity Theft Report: This report can help you create a recovery plan and provide proof to businesses and law enforcement. Visit IdentityTheft.gov to file a report and get personalized recovery steps.

Local Law Enforcement: Filing a police report can help in the investigation and provide documentation for your case. Be sure to provide as much information as possible, including any fraudulent transactions and correspondence.

Monitor your credit reports: Regularly check your credit reports for any signs of fraudulent activity. You are entitled to a free credit report from each of the major credit bureaus once a year at AnnualCreditReport.com.

Consider a credit freeze: This can prevent new accounts from being opened in your name without your permission. A credit freeze restricts access to your credit report, making it more difficult for identity thieves to open new accounts.

Use identity theft protection services: These services can provide additional monitoring and recovery assistance. Some services offer insurance to cover costs associated with identity theft recovery.

Resources and Support Systems

IdentityTheft.gov: The FTC's website offers a comprehensive recovery plan and resources. It provides step-by-step guidance on what to do if you become a victim of identity theft.

Credit Bureaus: Equifax, Experian, and TransUnion provide tools for monitoring and protecting your credit. They offer services such as credit monitoring, fraud alerts, and credit freezes.

Legal Aid: Organizations like Legal Aid provide free or low-cost legal assistance to victims of identity theft. They can help you navigate the legal complexities and recover from identity theft.

As technology advances, so do the methods used by identity thieves. Emerging threats include the use of artificial intelligence (AI) to create convincing phishing scams and deepfakes, which can manipulate audio and video to impersonate individuals. These new techniques make it even more challenging to distinguish between legitimate and fraudulent communications.

Advanced encryption: Improved encryption methods can protect personal data from being accessed by unauthorized parties. Encryption ensures that even if data is intercepted, it cannot be read without the proper decryption key.

Biometric authentication: Using fingerprints, facial recognition, or other biometric data can provide an additional layer of security. Biometric authentication is more difficult to replicate than traditional passwords.

Blockchain technology: This decentralized approach can enhance the security and transparency of transactions. Blockchain technology can provide a tamper-proof record of transactions, making it more difficult for identity thieves to alter data.

Experts predict that identity theft will continue to evolve, with cybercriminals finding new ways to exploit technological advancements. Staying informed and vigilant will be crucial for individuals and organizations alike. It is essential to keep up with the latest security practices and be proactive in protecting personal information.

Identity theft is a serious and evolving threat that can have significant consequences. By understanding the history, methods, and prevention strategies, individuals can better protect themselves and their personal information. Regularly monitoring your financial accounts, being cautious with personal information, and staying informed about new threats are essential steps in safeguarding your identity.

Vigilance is key to preventing identity theft. Regularly monitoring your financial accounts, being cautious with personal information, and staying informed about new threats are essential steps in safeguarding your identity. By taking proactive measures and staying informed, you can reduce the risk of becoming a victim of identity theft.

Encouragement to Spread Awareness

Raising awareness about identity theft is crucial. Share what you've learned with friends, family, and colleagues to help others protect themselves from this growing threat. The more people are informed and vigilant, the harder it becomes for identity thieves to succeed.

Appendix

Glossary of Terms

Phishing: A scam where fraudsters send emails or messages pretending to be from reputable companies to steal personal information.

Fraud Alert: A notice placed on your credit report to alert creditors of potential fraud.

Credit Freeze: A security measure that restricts access to your credit report, making it more difficult for identity thieves to open new accounts.

Chapter 8: Rise of Online Shopping Scams

The internet revolutionized the way we shop, offering unprecedented convenience and access to a global marketplace from the comfort of our homes. What began as a novel idea in the mid-1990s quickly transformed into a multi-billion-dollar industry. With giants like Amazon and eBay leading the charge, online shopping became a staple of modern life.

Online shopping offers numerous benefits, such as avoiding crowded stores, accessing a wider range of products, and enjoying the ease of having purchases delivered directly to your door. However, this convenience comes with its own set of risks. As online shopping became more prevalent, so did the opportunities for scammers to exploit unsuspecting consumers.

Importance of Understanding Online Shopping Scams

While the internet has made shopping easier, it has also opened new avenues for scammers. Online shopping scams are a significant threat, capable of causing financial loss and emotional distress. For beginners, understanding these scams is crucial to protect oneself and enjoy the benefits of e-commerce safely.

Online scams can range from simple phishing attempts to complex schemes involving fake websites and identity theft. Being aware of these threats and knowing how to avoid them can save you from potential headaches and financial losses.

Objectives of the Book

Educate readers about the history and evolution of online shopping scams

Provide detailed accounts of famous scams to illustrate common tactics used by fraudsters

Offer practical advice on how to avoid falling victim to scams

Share real-life case studies to highlight the impact of scams and lessons learned

Guide readers on the steps to take if they become a victim of online fraud

Early Days of Online Shopping

The concept of online shopping emerged in the early 1990s, with companies like Amazon and eBay pioneering the field. Initially, there was a lot of skepticism about entering credit card information online. Early adopters of e-commerce had to overcome the fear of their financial information being stolen.

In these early days, the primary concern was the lack of trust in the security of online transactions. Consumers were hesitant to provide their credit card details, fearing that they might be stolen and misused. Despite these fears, the convenience of shopping from home began to win over consumers.

Evolution of Online Scams

As online shopping grew, so did the ingenuity of scammers. Early scams were relatively simple, often involving fraudulent emails or fake auction listings. Over time, these scams have become more sophisticated, incorporating advanced techniques like phishing, malware, and elaborate fake websites.

The early scams often involved sending emails that appeared to be from legitimate companies, asking users to click on a link and enter their personal information. These phishing emails were designed to look convincing, with official logos and professional language. However, as consumers became more aware of these tactics, scammers evolved their methods.

Key Milestones in the Development of Online Theft

1990s: Introduction of online marketplaces, leading to initial forms of online fraud.

Early 2000s: Rise of phishing scams targeting online shoppers.

2010s: Emergence of complex scams involving fake e-commerce sites and social media platforms.

2020s: Increase in AI-driven scams and personalized phishing attacks.

Each of these milestones represents a significant step in the evolution of online shopping scams. As technology advances, so do the tactics of scammers. It is crucial for consumers to stay informed about the latest threats and how to protect themselves.

The eBay Phishing Scam

One of the most notorious scams involved phishing emails purportedly from eBay. These emails directed users to a fake eBay login page, where they would unwittingly enter their credentials. Scammers would then use this information to make unauthorized purchases or sell it on the dark web.

This scam was particularly effective because it capitalized on the trust that users had in eBay. The emails looked legitimate, complete with eBay logos and branding. Once users entered their login details on the fake page, scammers could access their accounts and make purchases, leaving the victims to deal with the financial fallout.

The Amazon Gift Card Scam

Another prevalent scam involved fraudulent Amazon gift cards. Scammers would offer these cards at a significant discount on third-party websites. Once purchased, victims would find that the cards were either invalid or already used. This scam exploited the trust people had in a well-known brand like Amazon.

In many cases, these fake gift cards were sold through social media ads or dubious websites. The promise of a great deal enticed many shoppers to buy them, only to be disappointed when they tried to use the cards. This scam highlights the importance of purchasing gift cards only from reputable sources.

Fake Retail Websites

Fake retail websites are a common scam tactic. These sites often mimic legitimate online stores, complete with convincing product photos and fake customer reviews. Shoppers who make purchases on these sites never receive their items, and their payment information is often stolen.

These fake websites are designed to look as authentic as possible, sometimes even copying the design and layout of real stores. Scammers use these sites to collect payment information, which they can then use for fraudulent purposes. Consumers may not realize they've been scammed until they never receive their order or notice unauthorized charges on their credit cards.

Recognizing Red Flags

To avoid online shopping scams, it's essential to recognize the warning signs:

Unusually Low Prices: If a deal seems too good to be true, it probably is. Scammers often lure victims with unbelievably low prices.

Poor Website Design: Legitimate sites invest in professional design. Shoddy design, poor grammar, and spelling mistakes are red flags.

Lack of Contact Information: Reputable retailers provide clear contact information, including a physical address and customer service number. The absence of this can indicate a scam.

By being aware of these red flags, you can avoid many common scams. Always take a moment to critically evaluate a website before making a purchase.

Best Practices for Safe Online Shopping

Secure Payment Methods: Use credit cards or payment services like PayPal that offer buyer protection. Avoid using debit cards or bank transfers for online purchases.

Checking for Secure Websites (HTTPS): Always shop on sites with HTTPS in the URL, indicating a secure connection. Look for the padlock symbol in the address bar.

Reading Reviews and Ratings: Look for reviews on independent platforms. Be wary of sites with only positive reviews, as these could be fake.

Following these best practices can significantly reduce your risk of falling victim to online shopping scams. Always prioritize security and take steps to verify the legitimacy of a website before entering your payment information.

Tools and Resources

Anti-Phishing Software: Tools like Norton and McAfee can help detect and block phishing attempts.

Browser Extensions: Extensions like Web of Trust (WOT) can alert you to potentially unsafe sites.

Official Government and Non-Profit Resources: Websites like the Federal Trade Commission (FTC) provide valuable information on avoiding scams.

Utilizing these tools and resources can provide an additional layer of protection against online scams. Regularly updating your software and staying informed about the latest threats can help you shop online with confidence.

Case Study 1: Jane's Story – Falling for a Fake Designer Bag

Jane, an avid online shopper, came across a website offering designer handbags at a fraction of the retail price. The site looked professional, and the reviews seemed genuine. Excited by the bargain, she purchased a bag. Weeks passed, and the bag never arrived. When she tried to contact customer service, she found the phone number and email were fake. Jane learned the hard way about the risks of deals that seem too good to be true.

Jane's story highlights the importance of thoroughly researching a website before making a purchase. Despite the professional appearance of the site, there were subtle red flags that she overlooked. This experience taught her to be more cautious and to verify the legitimacy of online retailers.

Case Study 2: Mike's Ordeal – The Too-Good-to-Be-True Smartphone Deal

Mike saw an ad on social media for a brand-new smartphone at half the usual price. The site appeared legitimate, and the payment process seemed secure. However, after making the purchase, he received a confirmation email that looked suspicious. Upon closer inspection, he realized the email contained numerous grammatical errors. Mike contacted his bank immediately and was able to cancel the transaction before it was too late.

Mike's quick thinking and attention to detail helped him avoid significant financial loss. This case study underscores the importance of scrutinizing confirmation emails and other communications from online sellers. If something seems off, it's better to err on the side of caution.

Case Study 3: The Anonymous – Identity Theft Through Online Shopping

A frequent online shopper, who preferred to remain anonymous, noticed unusual charges on their credit card statement. After investigating, they discovered that their personal information had been stolen through a fake e-commerce site. The scammers used their details to make numerous purchases, resulting in a long and stressful process to regain control of their identity and finances.

This case study emphasizes the severe consequences of identity theft. Recovering from such an incident can be a lengthy and challenging process. It highlights the importance of monitoring your financial statements and acting quickly if you notice any suspicious activity.

Immediate Steps to Take

If you suspect you've fallen victim to an online shopping scam, act quickly:

Contact Your Bank: Report the fraudulent transaction to your bank or credit card company to block further unauthorized charges.

Report the Scam: File a report with your local consumer protection agency or the Federal Trade Commission (FTC).

Taking these immediate steps can help minimize the damage and prevent further unauthorized transactions. It's crucial to act promptly and follow the necessary procedures to protect your finances.

Long-Term Strategies for Recovery

Monitoring Your Credit Report: Regularly check your credit report for any unauthorized activity. You can obtain free reports from major credit bureaus.

Using Identity Theft Protection Services: Consider enrolling in a service that monitors your personal information and alerts you to potential fraud.

Long-term vigilance is essential to ensure that scammers do not continue to exploit your information. By monitoring your credit and utilizing protection services, you can safeguard against future threats.

Emotional Impact and Seeking Support

Being scammed can be a traumatic experience. It's essential to address the emotional impact:

Talk to Someone: Share your experience with friends or family. Talking about it can help alleviate some of the stress and anxiety.

Seek Professional Help: Consider counseling if the experience significantly impacts your mental health.

Recovering from a scam involves more than just financial recovery. It's important to take care of your mental and emotional well-being. Don't hesitate to seek support if you need it.

Online shopping scams are a real and growing threat. By understanding the history, recognizing common scams, and following best practices, you can protect yourself from becoming a victim.

In this chapter, we explored the evolution of online shopping scams, highlighted some of the most notorious scams, provided practical advice on how to avoid them, and shared real-life case studies to illustrate the impact of these scams.

Encouragement to Stay Vigilant

Stay informed and vigilant. The landscape of online shopping is continually evolving, and so are the tactics of scammers.

By staying informed and adopting safe online shopping practices, you can enjoy the convenience of e-commerce without falling prey to scams. Remember to trust your instincts and always prioritize your security.

The future of online shopping looks promising with advancements in security technologies. However, personal vigilance remains the best defense against online scams.

As technology continues to advance, we can expect new and innovative security measures to be developed. However, scammers will also continue to evolve their tactics. By staying educated and cautious, you can navigate the world of online shopping safely and confidently.

References

Federal Trade Commission (FTC) website

Norton Anti-Phishing resources

McAfee Phishing and Scam Protection tools

Web of Trust (WOT) browser extension

Various articles and reports on online shopping scams

Chapter 9: Pyramid Schemes

The concept of pyramid schemes dates back centuries, but their modern form began to take shape in the early 20th century. One of the earliest and most infamous examples is the scheme operated by Charles Ponzi in the 1920s. Ponzi promised investors a 50% return on their investment within 45 days, allegedly by exploiting international postal reply coupons. In reality, Ponzi used the money from new investors to pay off earlier investors, creating an illusion of a profitable business. The scheme eventually collapsed, leading to significant financial losses for those involved and coining the term "Ponzi scheme."

In the decades that followed, pyramid schemes evolved, adapting to changing economic landscapes and regulatory environments. The 1970s and 1980s saw a surge in multi-level marketing (MLM) companies, some of which blurred the lines between legitimate business practices and fraudulent schemes. Regulatory bodies around the world began to crack down on these operations, leading to numerous legal battles and the development of stricter laws aimed at protecting consumers.

Despite these efforts, pyramid schemes have persisted into the 21st century, often disguised as investment opportunities, online businesses, or network marketing ventures. The rise of the internet and social media has provided new avenues for promoters to reach potential victims, making it more important than ever for individuals to be vigilant and informed.

At its core, a pyramid scheme is a business model that recruits members via a promise of payments or services for enrolling others into the scheme, rather than supplying investments or sale of products. The hallmark of these schemes is the emphasis on recruitment over product sales or legitimate business operations.

Typically, participants are required to make an initial investment or purchase a product package. They are then encouraged to recruit others to do the same, with the promise of earning commissions or bonuses based on the number of new recruits they bring in. This creates a pyramid-like structure, where the majority of the money flows to the top tiers of the pyramid, leaving those at the bottom with little to no return on their investment.

One key difference between pyramid schemes and legitimate multi-level marketing (MLM) companies is the focus on product sales. While MLMs generate revenue primarily through the sale of actual products or services, pyramid schemes rely heavily on recruitment fees. Additionally, in a legitimate MLM, there is typically an emphasis on training and support for sales representatives, along with a sustainable compensation plan that rewards product sales over recruitment.

Charles Ponzi and the Original Ponzi Scheme

Charles Ponzi's scheme in the early 20th century remains one of the most famous examples of a pyramid scheme. Promising investors extraordinary returns through a convoluted system of international postal coupons, Ponzi attracted millions of dollars. However, the scheme was unsustainable, as Ponzi used the funds from new investors to pay earlier investors. When the scheme collapsed, it left thousands of people in financial ruin and Ponzi in prison.

Bernie Madoff's Ponzi Scheme

Decades later, Bernie Madoff operated one of the largest and most devastating Ponzi schemes in history. Madoff, a well-respected figure in the financial world, promised steady, high returns through what he claimed were sophisticated trading strategies. In reality, Madoff was using new investors' funds to pay returns to earlier investors, creating an illusion of profitability. When the scheme unraveled in 2008, it resulted in an estimated $65 billion in losses, affecting thousands of investors, from individuals to charitable organizations.

Other Notable Pyramid Schemes

BurnLounge: A music distribution company that was shut down by the Federal Trade Commission (FTC) in 2007 for operating a pyramid scheme. BurnLounge recruited individuals to sell music online, but the primary focus was on recruiting others to buy into the business, rather than selling music.

Fortune Hi-Tech Marketing: Another MLM company that was shut down by the FTC in 2013 for operating a pyramid scheme. The company claimed to sell various services and products, but most of the revenue came from recruiting new members who paid for the privilege of joining.

Red Flags and Warning Signs

Recognizing a pyramid scheme can be challenging, especially when promoters are skilled at disguising their operations as legitimate business opportunities. However, there are several red flags that can help you identify a potential pyramid scheme:

Emphasis on Recruitment: If the primary focus is on recruiting new members rather than selling a product or service, it is likely a pyramid scheme.

High Upfront Costs: Be wary of opportunities that require significant upfront investments or the purchase of expensive product packages.

Promise of High Returns with Little Effort: If the scheme promises substantial returns with minimal effort, it is likely too good to be true.

Complex Commission Structures: Pyramid schemes often have convoluted commission structures designed to confuse and entice recruits.

Questions to Ask Before Investing

What is the product or service being sold, and is there a genuine demand for it?

How are commissions earned, and is recruitment the primary way to make money?

What is the company's track record, and are there any legal actions or complaints against it?

Can you easily contact current and former members to get their honest feedback?

Tips for Protecting Yourself

Conduct thorough research before investing in any opportunity.

Seek advice from trusted financial advisors or professionals.

Be cautious of high-pressure sales tactics and urgent recruitment pitches.

Trust your instincts; if something feels off, it probably is.

Pyramid schemes can have devastating financial impacts on individuals, often resulting in significant losses and debt. Those who join these schemes in the hopes of quick riches may find themselves out of pocket and struggling to recover their investments.

The social and psychological effects can be equally damaging. Participants may experience feelings of betrayal, guilt, and shame, particularly if they have recruited friends or family members who also lose money. The sense of community and belonging that pyramid schemes often create can quickly turn into isolation and distrust when the scheme collapses.

On a broader scale, pyramid schemes can undermine trust in legitimate businesses and financial systems, leading to a more cautious and skeptical public. This can make it more challenging for genuine enterprises to gain the trust and support of potential customers and investors.

Case Study: Herbalife

Herbalife, a global nutrition company, has faced numerous accusations of operating as a pyramid scheme. Critics argue that the company's compensation plan relies heavily on recruitment rather than product sales, leading to significant financial losses for many distributors. In 2016, Herbalife settled with the FTC, agreeing to restructure its business practices and pay $200 million to distributors who had lost money.

Case Study: Vemma Nutrition Company

Vemma, another MLM company, was accused by the FTC in 2015 of operating a pyramid scheme. The company recruited young people with promises of financial independence and lavish lifestyles, but most participants ended up losing money. The FTC's action resulted in a $238 million settlement and significant changes to Vemma's business model.

Lessons Learned

Herbalife: The importance of a balanced business model that prioritizes product sales over recruitment.

Vemma: The need for regulatory oversight and consumer education to prevent exploitation, especially of vulnerable populations.

Pyramid schemes are a persistent threat in the world of business and investment, preying on the hopes and aspirations of individuals seeking financial freedom. By understanding the history, identifying the red flags, and learning from past case studies, you can protect yourself and others from falling victim to these fraudulent schemes. Stay informed, ask the right questions, and always approach new opportunities with a healthy dose of skepticism. Remember, if something sounds too good to be true, it probably is.

Chapter 10: Romance Scams

In the digital age, the quest for love has expanded beyond traditional boundaries, introducing new opportunities and, unfortunately, new risks. Romance scams, a sinister form of fraud, prey on the vulnerabilities of those seeking companionship. This book aims to shed light on the shadowy world of romance scams, offering insights into their history, famous cases, and practical advice on how to avoid falling victim. Whether you're a seasoned internet user or new to online dating, this guide is designed to equip you with the knowledge to recognize and protect yourself from these deceitful schemes.

As we delve into the world of romance scams, it's essential to understand that these scams can happen to anyone, regardless of age, gender, or background. Scammers are skilled at manipulating emotions and creating believable stories that make their targets feel special and loved. This book will provide you with the tools to identify, avoid, and protect yourself from these fraudulent activities. By staying informed and vigilant, you can navigate the online dating world safely and confidently.

Romance scams are not a new phenomenon. Their roots can be traced back to times when love letters were the primary means of long-distance communication. In the early 20th century, scammers would place personal ads in newspapers, targeting lonely hearts with promises of affection and marriage, only to disappear after receiving money.

Early Examples of Romance Scams

In the early days, romance scams were relatively low-tech. One classic example involved "lonely hearts" ads in newspapers. Scammers would place ads looking for companionship, correspond with their targets via letters, and then concoct stories of financial distress or travel expenses to solicit money. These schemes relied on the emotional connection built through letters and promises of a future together.

The Evolution with Technology

With the advent of the internet in the late 20th century, romance scams took on new dimensions. Email and chat rooms became breeding grounds for fraudsters. The Nigerian Prince scam, one of the earliest forms of internet fraud, often included elements of romantic manipulation to elicit funds from unsuspecting victims.

As social media platforms and online dating sites gained popularity in the 21st century, scammers found fertile ground for their operations. These platforms allowed them to create elaborate fake profiles, building trust over time before making their move. The anonymity and vast reach of the internet made it easier for scammers to target individuals globally, leading to a surge in reported cases of romance scams.

Major Milestones in Romance Scams

The 2000s saw a significant increase in romance scams as online dating became more popular. Scammers began using dating websites to create fake profiles, luring victims with attractive photos and sweet messages. As technology advanced, so did the sophistication of these scams. Scammers started using video calls with doctored videos, fake social media accounts, and even sending small gifts to build credibility. This period also saw the rise of organized scam rings, often based in countries like Nigeria, Ghana, and the Philippines, where groups of scammers would work together to defraud victims.

One of the most infamous romance scams involved a woman named Mary, who believed she had found love with a man claiming to be a U.S. soldier stationed overseas. Over two years, Mary sent over $100,000 to help him with various emergencies. When the truth was uncovered, it was revealed that the soldier never existed; Mary had been corresponding with a group of scammers based in Nigeria.

Notable Cases and Their Impacts

Mary and the Soldier: Mary's story is a heartbreaking example of how scammers exploit emotions. She met "John" on a dating site, and their relationship quickly intensified. John claimed to be a U.S. soldier stationed in Afghanistan. He sent pictures, shared personal stories, and after several months, he started asking for money. First, it was for a leave application, then medical emergencies, and eventually, a transfer fee to come home. Mary sent her life savings, only to realize she had been scammed. The psychological and financial impact on her was devastating, leading to depression and financial hardship.

The Sweetheart Swindler: Another infamous case involved a man who targeted elderly women. He would woo them, gain their trust, and convince them to marry him. Once married, he would drain their bank accounts and disappear. His charm and elaborate lies left a trail of financially ruined and emotionally scarred victims. This case highlights how scammers can manipulate not just through digital means but also in real-life interactions.

Analysis of How These Scams Were Perpetrated

These scams often follow a pattern: initial contact through a dating site or social media, followed by a period of intense communication to build trust. Scammers use flattery, feigned vulnerability, and fabricated stories to create an emotional bond. Once trust is established, they invent crises that require financial assistance. Common scenarios include medical emergencies, legal troubles, or travel expenses. The scammer may use fake documents, photos, and even accomplices to make their stories more convincing.

By understanding these patterns, individuals can better recognize the warning signs and avoid falling into the same traps. It's important to remember that anyone can be a target, and staying informed is the first line of defense against these deceptive schemes.

Understanding the common tactics used by romance scammers is crucial in protecting oneself. Here are some red flags and practical tips to help you stay safe:

Common Tactics Used by Scammers

Too Good to Be True: Scammers often create profiles of exceptionally attractive and successful individuals.

Rapid Declaration of Love: Be wary of someone who professes love quickly.

Inconsistent Stories: Pay attention to inconsistencies in their stories or background.

Requests for Money: Any request for financial assistance, regardless of the reason, is a major red flag.

Practical Tips to Stay Safe

Verify Their Identity: Use reverse image searches and look for inconsistencies in their profile.

Keep Personal Information Private: Avoid sharing sensitive information early in the relationship.

Report Suspicious Activity: Report any suspicious profiles to the dating site or social media platform.

Stay Informed: Educate yourself about the latest scams and tactics used by fraudsters.

Online Resources and Tools

Scam Awareness Websites: Websites like Scamwatch and the Better Business Bureau offer valuable information and resources.

Verification Services: Services that can help verify the identity of someone you're communicating with online.

Support Networks: Online forums and support groups for victims of romance scams.

Red Flags to Watch Out For

Inconsistent Information: If their stories don't add up or they are reluctant to provide verifiable details.

Avoiding In-Person Meetings: Making excuses to avoid video calls or face-to-face meetings is a major warning sign.

Quickly Moving Off Platform: Wanting to switch from the dating site to personal email or messaging apps early on.

Sudden Financial Requests: Any request for money, no matter how plausible it sounds, should be met with skepticism.

Real-life stories provide valuable lessons and insights into the world of romance scams. Here are a few case studies:

Case Study 1: Sarah's Story

Sarah met "David" on a popular dating site. After months of daily communication, David claimed he needed money for a business emergency. Sarah, believing in their relationship, sent him $5,000. David vanished shortly after, leaving Sarah heartbroken and financially strained. Sarah's case highlights the importance of not sending money to someone you've never met in person and the emotional toll these scams can take.

Case Study 2: John's Experience

John was approached by "Linda" on social media. Over several months, Linda built a convincing story about her life and even sent John small gifts. Eventually, she asked for money to help her with a legal issue. John, suspecting something was amiss, reported her profile. It was discovered that "Linda" was part of an organized crime ring. This case emphasizes the importance of trusting your instincts and verifying information.

Lessons Learned from These Cases

Verify Before Trusting: Always verify the identity of the person you are communicating with.

Beware of Emotional Manipulation: Scammers often play on emotions to elicit sympathy and trust.

Report Suspicious Activities: Reporting can prevent others from falling victim.

Romance scams exploit our most human desire: the need for connection and love. By staying informed and vigilant, we can protect ourselves and others from falling victim to these deceitful schemes. Remember to trust your instincts, verify identities, and never hesitate to report suspicious activities. Awareness and education are our best defenses against romance scams. Spread the word, share this knowledge, and help create a safer online community for everyone.

Navigating the world of online dating can be challenging, but with the right knowledge and precautions, you can protect yourself from romance scams. Remember, genuine love and connection do not come with demands for money or secrecy. Stay safe, stay informed, and trust your instincts. By doing so, you can enjoy the benefits of online dating while avoiding the pitfalls of romance scams.

Part 2: The Greatest Scams in History

The following are the 10 scams that are recognized as the greatest in history

Chapter 11: The South Sea Bubble

In the early 18th century, England was a nation of merchants, traders, and investors, eager to expand their fortunes. Against this backdrop emerged one of the most infamous financial disasters in history: the South Sea Bubble. This event, marked by extreme speculation and financial greed, ultimately led to the ruin of many investors and significant changes in financial regulation. This book explores the South Sea Bubble, from its origins and rise to its catastrophic fall and lasting impact.

To understand the South Sea Bubble, we need to delve into the economic and political landscape of early 18th century Britain. The South Sea Company was founded in 1711, during a time of war and economic uncertainty. The government was burdened with massive debt from the War of Spanish Succession, and the South Sea Company was created as a solution to manage and reduce this debt. In exchange for taking on the national debt, the company was granted exclusive trading rights with Spanish colonies in South America, a prospect that seemed full of promise.

However, the reality was far less lucrative than anticipated. The Spanish colonies were not as open to British traders as hoped, and the company's trading prospects were limited. Despite this, the company managed to present itself as an incredibly profitable venture, fueling speculation and excitement among investors.

The early successes of the South Sea Company, coupled with clever marketing and the allure of vast profits, led to a rapid rise in its stock prices. The company and its promoters used a variety of tactics to inflate the perceived value of its shares. They promised extravagant returns, paid handsome dividends from borrowed money, and manipulated public perception through rumors and strategic investments by influential figures.

As the stock prices soared, a frenzy of public speculation ensued. Everyone, from wealthy aristocrats to common shopkeepers, wanted a piece of the action. People mortgaged their homes and borrowed heavily to buy shares, driven by the fear of missing out on the fortunes that seemed within reach. The government, too, was swept up in the excitement, with members of Parliament investing heavily.

The bubble reached its peak in the summer of 1720. The stock price of the South Sea Company had skyrocketed, and the frenzy of speculation reached unprecedented levels. However, the rapid rise in stock prices was unsustainable. The reality of the company's limited trading success began to surface, and confidence started to wane.

Key figures, such as John Blunt, who orchestrated much of the company's strategy, began to sell their shares quietly, signaling the impending collapse. As news of insider selling and the company's shaky foundations spread, panic set in. Investors rushed to sell their shares, leading to a rapid and catastrophic decline in stock prices. By the end of 1720, the South Sea Bubble had burst, leaving countless investors in financial ruin.

The collapse of the South Sea Bubble had profound immediate and long-term consequences. Financially, many investors lost their entire fortunes, and the economic impact was severe. Politically, the scandal led to a crisis of confidence in the government and its handling of economic affairs. Several high-profile figures were implicated, and there were calls for accountability and reform.

In the wake of the collapse, there were significant changes in economic policy and market regulation. The government introduced measures to restore confidence in the financial system and prevent such speculative bubbles in the future. The Bubble Act of 1720, which restricted the formation of joint-stock companies without a royal charter, was one such measure aimed at curbing speculative mania.

The South Sea Bubble serves as a powerful reminder of the dangers of unchecked speculation and financial greed. It highlights the importance of transparency, regulation, and investor education in maintaining a stable financial system. The lessons learned from this event are still relevant today, as modern financial markets continue to grapple with similar challenges. By understanding the history of the South Sea Bubble, we can better appreciate the complexities of financial markets and the need for prudent investment practices.

Chapter 12: The Ponzi Scheme (1920)

In the annals of financial fraud, few names stand out as prominently as Charles Ponzi. The Ponzi Scheme, named after him, is a type of scam that promises high returns with little risk to investors. This book delves into the origins, mechanics, and ultimate downfall of the original Ponzi Scheme, providing insights into how such schemes work and the lessons we can learn to protect ourselves today.

Charles Ponzi was an Italian immigrant who arrived in the United States in 1903, seeking fortune and success. His early years were marked by a series of failed ventures, but he eventually stumbled upon an idea that he believed would make him rich beyond his wildest dreams.

The economic environment of post-World War I America was ripe for opportunity and speculation. With the economy recovering and people eager to invest, Ponzi saw his chance. He devised a scheme based on the arbitrage of international reply coupons, which were used for postage. Ponzi claimed he could buy these coupons cheaply in one country and redeem them for a profit in another, exploiting exchange rate differences.

Ponzi began his scheme in December 1919, offering investors a 50% return on investment in just 45 days. This extraordinary promise attracted a flood of investors, and word quickly spread. Ponzi's charm and confidence played a crucial role in convincing people to part with their money.

In reality, Ponzi was using the money from new investors to pay returns to earlier investors, creating the illusion of a profitable business. This method, now known as a Ponzi Scheme, relies on a constant influx of new investments to sustain payouts. As long as new money keeps coming in, the scheme appears successful.

Public reaction was overwhelmingly positive. Newspapers lauded Ponzi as a financial genius, and people from all walks of life invested their savings. The media coverage fueled further investment, creating a feedback loop that drove the scheme to unprecedented heights.

By mid-1920, Ponzi's scheme began to unravel. Investigations by journalists and the government revealed discrepancies in his operations. The Boston Post published a critical article, raising doubts about the legitimacy of Ponzi's business. This led to a run on his company as investors scrambled to withdraw their money.

The rapid withdrawal requests exposed Ponzi's inability to pay everyone back, leading to his arrest on August 12, 1920. Legal actions followed, and Ponzi was charged with multiple counts of mail fraud. He was eventually sentenced to prison, serving several years behind bars.

The impact on investors was devastating. Many lost their life savings, and the collapse of the scheme shook public confidence in financial institutions. The Ponzi Scheme had highlighted the need for better regulatory oversight and investor protection.

After serving his prison sentence, Ponzi attempted various other schemes, but none matched the scale of his original fraud. He eventually died in poverty, but his name lived on as a synonym for financial deceit.

The long-term effects of the Ponzi Scheme were significant. It led to increased regulation of financial markets and greater scrutiny of investment schemes. The Securities and Exchange Commission (SEC) was established in part to prevent such frauds and protect investors.

Understanding why the scheme succeeded and failed is crucial. Ponzi's ability to exploit human greed and the lack of regulatory oversight were key factors. His scheme serves as a cautionary tale about the dangers of investments that seem too good to be true.

The story of Charles Ponzi and his infamous scheme is a reminder of the perils of financial fraud. It underscores the importance of skepticism, due diligence, and regulatory frameworks in protecting investors. By learning from the past, we can better safeguard ourselves against similar scams in the future.

Chapter 13: The Enron Scandal (2001)

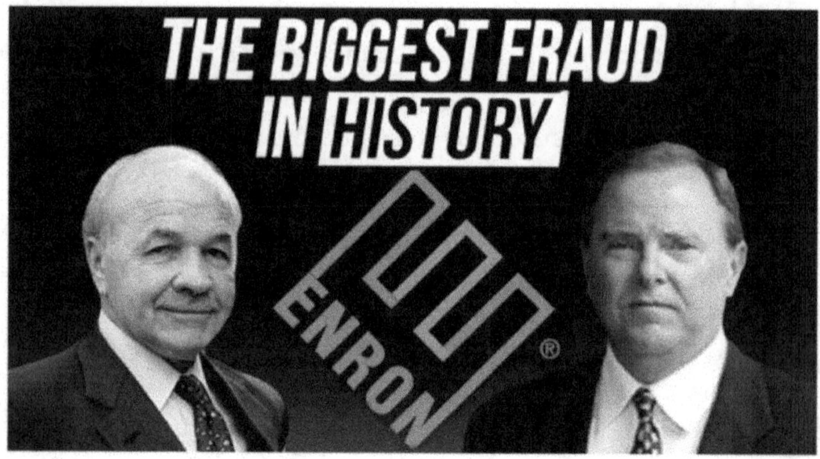

The Enron scandal, one of the most notorious cases of corporate fraud in history, brought down one of America's largest companies and led to widespread regulatory reforms. This book explores the rise and fall of Enron, the fraudulent practices that led to its collapse, and the lasting impact on corporate governance.

Enron was founded in 1985 through the merger of Houston Natural Gas and InterNorth. Under the leadership of Kenneth Lay, the company transformed from a traditional energy supplier into a diversified energy and commodities trading giant. The economic and regulatory environment of the 1990s, characterized by deregulation and market liberalization, provided fertile ground for Enron's rapid growth.

Key figures in the scandal included Kenneth Lay, CEO; Jeffrey Skilling, COO; and Andrew Fastow, CFO. These executives were instrumental in creating and perpetuating the fraudulent practices that would ultimately lead to Enron's downfall.

Enron's fraudulent practices were complex and multifaceted. The company used special purpose entities (SPEs) to hide debt and inflate profits, creating a misleading picture of financial health. These off-balance-sheet entities allowed Enron to keep substantial liabilities off its books while reporting impressive earnings.

The manipulation of financial statements was aided by complicity from auditors and banks. Arthur Andersen, Enron's auditing firm, failed to perform adequate audits and overlooked numerous red flags. Major banks also played a role by structuring the SPEs and facilitating questionable transactions.

Stories from within the company reveal a culture of aggressive risk-taking and ethical lapses. Employees were pressured to meet unrealistic targets, and dissent was discouraged. The pursuit of short-term profits overshadowed long-term sustainability, leading to a series of increasingly risky and deceptive practices.

The unraveling of Enron began in late 2001, when a series of articles and investigations exposed the company's dubious accounting practices. The revelation of hidden debt and inflated profits caused Enron's stock price to plummet, triggering panic among investors.

Legal and financial consequences swiftly followed. Enron filed for bankruptcy on December 2, 2001, marking the largest bankruptcy in U.S. history at the time. The collapse resulted in thousands of job losses and wiped out billions in shareholder value.

The impact on employees and investors was profound. Many employees lost their pensions, and investors saw their savings vanish. The scandal also led to a crisis of confidence in corporate governance and accounting practices.

The Enron scandal prompted significant regulatory changes aimed at preventing similar occurrences in the future. The Sarbanes-Oxley

Act of 2002 introduced stringent requirements for financial reporting, internal controls, and auditor independence.

Long-term impacts on corporate governance included increased scrutiny of executive compensation, greater transparency, and stronger accountability mechanisms. The scandal also underscored the importance of ethical leadership and corporate culture in ensuring sustainable business practices.

Analysis of the scandal's legacy reveals that while regulatory reforms have strengthened oversight, challenges remain. The lessons from Enron continue to be relevant as companies navigate the complexities of modern financial markets.

The Enron scandal is a stark reminder of the dangers of unchecked corporate greed and the importance of robust regulatory frameworks. By understanding the factors that led to Enron's downfall, we can better appreciate the need for ethical leadership and strong governance in the corporate world. The story of Enron serves as a cautionary tale for businesses and investors alike, highlighting the enduring relevance of integrity and accountability.

Chapter 14: The Bernie Madoff Ponzi Scheme (2008)

The Bernie Madoff Ponzi Scheme, one of the largest and most infamous financial frauds in history, shocked the world and left countless victims in its wake. This book examines the rise and fall of Bernie Madoff, the mechanics of his Ponzi Scheme, and the broader implications for financial regulation and investor protection.

Bernard "Bernie" Madoff was a well-respected financier and former chairman of the NASDAQ stock exchange. His investment firm, Bernard L. Madoff Investment Securities LLC, was founded in 1960 and became one of the most successful and trusted names on Wall Street.

The economic context of the early 2000s, characterized by rising markets and abundant liquidity, provided a favorable environment for Madoff's scheme. His reputation and connections in the financial world helped attract a steady stream of investors, including wealthy individuals, charities, and institutional investors.

Madoff's Ponzi Scheme promised consistent, high returns regardless of market conditions. He claimed to use a "split-strike conversion" strategy, which purportedly involved buying and selling stocks and options to generate profits. In reality, Madoff was using new investor money to pay returns to earlier investors, creating the illusion of a successful investment operation.

The scheme relied on Madoff's reputation and the trust he had built over decades. Many investors, including sophisticated institutions, failed to perform due diligence, relying instead on Madoff's assurances and the steady returns he delivered.

Warning signs were present but often overlooked. Some financial analysts and industry insiders raised doubts about Madoff's returns, but these concerns were dismissed or ignored. The lack of transparency and the firm's secrecy about its trading activities should have raised red flags.

The collapse of Madoff's scheme began in December 2008, when he confessed to his sons that his investment business was "one big lie." This admission led to his arrest and the subsequent unraveling of the scheme. The financial crisis of 2008, which led to increased withdrawal requests, had exposed the scheme's unsustainable nature.

Legal actions swiftly followed, with Madoff pleading guilty to 11 federal felonies, including securities fraud, wire fraud, and money laundering. He was sentenced to 150 years in prison, effectively a life sentence given his age.

The impact on victims was catastrophic. Many lost their life savings, and the total losses were estimated at around $65 billion, making it the largest Ponzi Scheme in history. The emotional and financial toll on victims was immense, with some losing not just their money but their trust in the financial system.

Efforts to recover assets and compensate victims have been ongoing. The Madoff Victim Fund and other recovery initiatives have managed to return some of the stolen funds, but many victims have only received a fraction of their losses.

The regulatory changes prompted by the scandal included increased scrutiny of investment advisors and stricter oversight by the Securities and Exchange Commission (SEC). The scandal exposed significant weaknesses in the regulatory framework, leading to calls for more robust investor protection measures.

The Madoff Ponzi Scheme also highlighted the importance of due diligence and skepticism in investing. It served as a stark reminder that even well-respected figures can perpetrate massive frauds, underscoring the need for transparency and accountability.

The Bernie Madoff Ponzi Scheme is a cautionary tale about the dangers of blind trust and the importance of regulatory oversight. By understanding the factors that enabled Madoff to perpetrate his fraud for so long, we can better appreciate the need for vigilance and skepticism in financial matters. The lessons from this scandal are crucial for investors and regulators alike, emphasizing the enduring relevance of integrity and transparency in the financial world.

Chapter 15: The Dutch Tulip Mania (1637)

The Dutch Tulip Mania of the 17th century is often cited as one of the earliest examples of a speculative bubble. This book explores the fascinating story of how tulip bulbs became the center of a financial frenzy, leading to one of the most famous market crashes in history. We'll delve into the economic, social, and cultural factors that fueled the mania and its lasting impact on financial markets.

The Dutch Golden Age was a period of great prosperity and cultural achievement in the Netherlands. The country's thriving economy was driven by trade, finance, and innovation. During this time, tulips, introduced from the Ottoman Empire, became highly prized for their beauty and rarity.

The initial stages of the tulip market were characterized by genuine interest and appreciation for the flowers. Tulips became a status symbol, and their cultivation and trade flourished. The economic environment of the time, with its burgeoning middle class and sophisticated financial infrastructure, set the stage for speculative activity.

The Bubble Forms

As the demand for tulips grew, prices began to rise. Speculative trading took hold, and the market dynamics shifted from genuine appreciation to profit-driven investment. People from all walks of life, including merchants, farmers, and artisans, were drawn into the frenzy, hoping to make quick profits.

The rise in tulip prices was fueled by a combination of factors, including the perception of scarcity, the allure of novelty, and the belief that prices would continue to climb. Tulip bulbs were traded at auctions, in taverns, and through informal networks, with prices reaching astonishing levels.

Stories from the period illustrate the extent of the speculation. Some individuals mortgaged their homes and sold valuable possessions to buy tulip bulbs, betting everything on the continued rise in prices. The frenzy reached its peak in the winter of 1636-1637, with certain rare bulbs selling for the equivalent of a house or more.

The turning point came in February 1637, when buyers suddenly stopped showing up at tulip auctions. Panic set in as people realized that the prices were unsustainable and began to sell their bulbs. The market crashed, and prices plummeted, leaving many investors in financial ruin.

The immediate financial and social impacts were severe. People who had invested heavily in tulips lost their fortunes, and the broader economy experienced a downturn. The collapse of the tulip market led to widespread disillusionment and a reevaluation of speculative practices.

Government and public reactions varied. In some cases, authorities attempted to mediate disputes and provide relief, while in others, they distanced themselves from the speculative excesses. The aftermath saw a push for greater regulation and caution in financial dealings.

Aftermath and Consequences

The long-term economic effects of the Tulip Mania were relatively contained, as the broader Dutch economy remained robust. However, the event had significant cultural and psychological impacts, shaping attitudes toward speculation and investment.

Historical interpretations of the Tulip Mania have varied, with some viewing it as a cautionary tale of irrational exuberance and others seeing it as a complex social phenomenon. The event has been studied extensively, offering valuable insights into the dynamics of speculative bubbles.

Comparisons with modern speculative bubbles, such as the dot-com bubble and the housing market crash, highlight the enduring relevance of the Tulip Mania. The lessons learned from this early bubble continue to inform financial regulation and investor behavior.

The Dutch Tulip Mania is a fascinating and instructive episode in financial history. It underscores the dangers of speculative excess and the importance of understanding market dynamics. By exploring this historical event, we gain valuable perspectives on the nature of financial bubbles and the need for prudent investment practices. The story of the Tulip Mania remains a compelling reminder of the timeless challenges and opportunities in the world of finance.

Chapter 16: The Savings and Loan Crisis (1980s)

The Savings and Loan Crisis of the 1980s was a major financial disaster that reshaped the American banking industry and led to significant regulatory changes. This book explores the origins, development, and aftermath of the crisis, providing insights into the factors that contributed to this unprecedented event and the lessons learned.

The Savings and Loan (S&L) industry, also known as thrifts, played a crucial role in American home financing for much of the 20th century. These institutions specialized in accepting savings deposits and making mortgage loans, contributing to the growth of homeownership.

The economic and regulatory environment of the late 1970s and early 1980s set the stage for the crisis. High inflation and interest rates, coupled with regulatory changes that allowed S&Ls to engage in riskier activities, created a volatile situation. The Depository Institutions Deregulation and Monetary Control Act of 1980 and the Garn-St. Germain Depository Institutions Act of 1982 were intended to help S&Ls compete, but they also removed many safeguards.

Early signs of trouble emerged as S&Ls faced increasing competition from other financial institutions and struggled with the mismatch between long-term, low-interest mortgage loans and short-term, high-interest deposits. The relaxation of regulatory oversight allowed many thrifts to pursue aggressive and speculative investments.

The crisis began to unfold in the early 1980s as more S&Ls became insolvent. Key events and major players included high-profile failures like Lincoln Savings and Loan, led by Charles Keating. Keating's aggressive investment strategies and fraudulent activities epitomized the excesses of the era.

Deregulation played a significant role in exacerbating the crisis. Without adequate oversight, many S&Ls engaged in high-risk investments in real estate, junk bonds, and other ventures that led to massive losses. The Federal Savings and Loan Insurance Corporation (FSLIC), which insured deposits, was overwhelmed by the number of failing institutions.

Government and industry responses were initially slow and inadequate. Efforts to stabilize the industry through bailouts and regulatory changes often fell short. The lack of timely intervention allowed the crisis to escalate, resulting in a greater number of failures and higher costs to taxpayers.

The peak of the crisis occurred in the late 1980s, with widespread failures and significant financial losses. By the time the crisis was fully addressed, over 1,000 S&Ls had failed, costing taxpayers an estimated $124 billion.

The financial and economic impacts were far-reaching. The collapse led to tighter credit conditions, reduced lending, and economic uncertainty. The broader banking industry was also affected, with increased scrutiny and regulatory pressure.

Legislative and regulatory responses included the establishment of the Resolution Trust Corporation (RTC) to manage and dispose of the assets of failed S&Ls. The Financial Institutions Reform, Recovery, and Enforcement Act (FIRREA) of 1989 introduced significant reforms aimed at preventing future crises and restoring confidence in the financial system.

The long-term consequences of the Savings and Loan Crisis were profound. The crisis reshaped the American financial landscape, leading to greater consolidation in the banking industry and stricter regulatory oversight. The lessons learned from the crisis influenced subsequent regulatory frameworks and financial practices.

Reforms and their effectiveness varied. While FIRREA and other measures helped stabilize the industry and prevent similar crises, challenges remained. The crisis underscored the importance of effective regulation, transparency, and risk management in the financial sector.

The Savings and Loan Crisis also highlighted the need for vigilance and accountability in the face of financial innovation and deregulation. The event remains a critical case study in the history of American finance, offering valuable lessons for policymakers, regulators, and investors.

The Savings and Loan Crisis of the 1980s serves as a stark reminder of the dangers of deregulation and excessive risk-taking in the financial sector. By understanding the factors that led to the crisis and the responses that followed, we can better appreciate the importance of prudent regulation and oversight. The lessons from this episode continue to inform modern financial policy and practice, emphasizing the need for balance between innovation and stability.

Chapter 17: The Bernie Ebbers and WorldCom Scandal (2002)

The WorldCom scandal, orchestrated by CEO Bernie Ebbers, is one of the largest accounting frauds in corporate history. This book delves into the rise and fall of WorldCom, the fraudulent practices that led to its collapse, and the broader implications for corporate governance and financial regulation.

WorldCom, founded in 1983, grew rapidly through a series of aggressive acquisitions, becoming one of the largest telecommunications companies in the world. Under the leadership of Bernie Ebbers, the company expanded its reach and market share, becoming a dominant player in the industry.

The economic and regulatory environment of the 1990s and early 2000s, characterized by the tech boom and deregulation, provided fertile ground for WorldCom's growth. The company's success was driven by its ability to capitalize on the booming demand for telecommunications and internet services.

Key figures involved in the scandal included Bernie Ebbers, CFO Scott Sullivan, and other top executives. These individuals were instrumental in the fraudulent activities that would eventually lead to WorldCom's downfall.

WorldCom's fraudulent practices centered on the manipulation of financial statements to inflate profits and hide expenses. The company used a variety of accounting tricks, including capitalizing operating expenses and booking bogus revenues, to present a false picture of financial health.

The manipulation of financial statements was facilitated by a lack of oversight and a culture of complicity within the company. Auditors and other external parties failed to detect or report the irregularities, allowing the fraud to continue unchecked.

Stories from within the company reveal a toxic corporate culture where dissent was discouraged, and ethical lapses were commonplace. Employees were pressured to meet unrealistic targets, leading to widespread manipulation of financial data.

The unraveling of WorldCom began in mid-2002, when internal audits and whistleblower reports exposed the extent of the accounting fraud. The revelation of nearly $4 billion in misreported expenses led to a swift decline in the company's stock price and investor confidence.

Legal and financial consequences followed, with WorldCom filing for bankruptcy on July 21, 2002. This marked the largest bankruptcy in U.S. history at the time, surpassing even the Enron scandal. The collapse resulted in significant financial losses for shareholders and employees.

The impact on employees and investors was devastating. Thousands of employees lost their jobs, and many investors saw their savings wiped out. The scandal also led to a broader crisis of confidence in corporate governance and accounting practices.

The WorldCom scandal prompted significant regulatory changes aimed at preventing similar occurrences in the future. The Sarbanes-Oxley Act of 2002 introduced stringent requirements for financial reporting, internal controls, and auditor independence, significantly reshaping corporate governance.

Long-term impacts on corporate governance included increased scrutiny of executive compensation, greater transparency, and stronger accountability mechanisms. The scandal underscored the importance of ethical leadership and corporate culture in ensuring sustainable business practices.

Analysis of the scandal's legacy reveals that while regulatory reforms have strengthened oversight, challenges remain. The lessons from WorldCom continue to be relevant as companies navigate the complexities of modern financial markets.

The WorldCom scandal is a stark reminder of the dangers of unchecked corporate greed and the importance of robust regulatory frameworks. By understanding the factors that led to WorldCom's downfall, we can better appreciate the need for ethical leadership and strong governance in the corporate world. The story of WorldCom serves as a cautionary tale for businesses and investors alike, highlighting the enduring relevance of integrity and accountability.

Chapter 18: The Bre-X Gold Scandal (1997)

The Bre-X Gold scandal, one of the most notorious mining frauds in history, captivated the world with its tale of greed, deception, and financial ruin. This book explores the rise and fall of Bre-X Minerals Ltd., the fraudulent practices that led to its collapse, and the broader implications for the mining industry and investor protection.

Bre-X Minerals Ltd., a small Canadian mining company, became the center of global attention in the mid-1990s when it announced the discovery of a massive gold deposit in Busang, Indonesia. The company's stock price soared as investors and mining experts alike were captivated by the promise of vast riches.

The economic and regulatory environment of the 1990s, characterized by high commodity prices and a favorable investment climate, provided a backdrop for Bre-X's rise. The company's success was driven by its ability to attract investment and generate excitement about its prospects.

Key figures involved in the scandal included David Walsh, Bre-X's founder and CEO; Michael de Guzman, the chief geologist; and John Felderhof, the exploration manager. These individuals played crucial roles in the fraudulent activities that would eventually lead to Bre-X's downfall.

The Fraud Unfolds

Bre-X's fraudulent practices centered on the falsification of gold assay results to inflate the perceived value of the Busang deposit. De Guzman and his team systematically "salted" drill samples with gold to create the illusion of a rich deposit, deceiving investors and experts alike.

The manipulation of assay results was facilitated by a lack of oversight and transparency in the mining industry. Bre-X's management, driven by greed and the desire to maintain investor confidence, perpetuated the fraud with the help of compliant laboratories and consultants.

Stories from within the company and the industry reveal a culture of deception and complicity. Many insiders were either unaware of the fraud or chose to ignore the red flags, blinded by the prospect of enormous profits.

The unraveling of Bre-X began in early 1997, when independent verification of the Busang deposit's gold content revealed that the samples had been tampered with. The revelation of the fraud led to a rapid decline in Bre-X's stock price and investor confidence.

Legal and financial consequences swiftly followed, with Bre-X filing for bankruptcy in 1997. The collapse resulted in significant financial losses for shareholders and investors, many of whom had been drawn in by the promise of spectacular returns.

The impact on the mining industry and investor confidence was profound. The scandal led to increased scrutiny of mining practices and a reevaluation of the due diligence processes employed by investors and analysts.

The Bre-X scandal prompted significant regulatory changes aimed at improving transparency and accountability in the mining industry. The introduction of the National Instrument 43-101 in Canada, which established standards for the disclosure of mineral project information, was a direct response to the scandal.

Long-term consequences for the mining sector included greater emphasis on independent verification and more rigorous reporting standards. The scandal also highlighted the importance of ethical practices and investor protection in the industry.

Analysis of the scandal's legacy reveals that while regulatory reforms have strengthened oversight, challenges remain. The lessons from Bre-X continue to be relevant as the mining industry navigates the complexities of modern exploration and investment.

The Bre-X Gold scandal serves as a powerful reminder of the dangers of unchecked greed and the importance of transparency and accountability in the mining industry. By understanding the factors that led to Bre-X's downfall, we can better appreciate the need for rigorous due diligence and ethical practices. The story of Bre-X remains a cautionary tale for investors and industry professionals alike, emphasizing the enduring relevance of integrity and oversight.

Chapter 19: The Fyre Festival Fraud (2017)

The Fyre Festival fraud, one of the most infamous event planning disasters in recent history, exposed the dark side of social media hype and unfulfilled promises. This book explores the rise and fall of the Fyre Festival, the fraudulent practices that led to its collapse, and the broader implications for event planning and marketing.

The Fyre Festival was conceived by Billy McFarland and rapper Ja Rule as a luxurious music festival set on a private island in the Bahamas. Marketed as an exclusive event with top-tier musical acts, gourmet food, and lavish accommodations, the festival quickly garnered attention from social media influencers and celebrities.

The economic and social media environment of the late 2010s, characterized by the rise of influencer marketing and the power of social media, provided a backdrop for the festival's rapid growth. The promise of a once-in-a-lifetime experience attracted a large number of ticket buyers, eager to be part of the exclusive event.

Key figures involved in the scandal included Billy McFarland, the festival's founder and CEO; Ja Rule, the celebrity co-founder; and a host of social media influencers who promoted the event. These individuals played crucial roles in the promotion and execution of the festival.

The fraudulent practices behind the Fyre Festival centered on misleading marketing and the failure to deliver on promises. The festival's promotional materials featured luxurious accommodations, gourmet meals, and top-tier entertainment, none of which were adequately planned or provided.

The manipulation of social media and influencer marketing played a significant role in creating the illusion of a high-end event. Influencers were paid to promote the festival without fully understanding the reality of the situation, leading to widespread misinformation and unrealistic expectations.

Stories from within the organization reveal a chaotic and mismanaged planning process. Despite numerous warnings and signs of impending failure, McFarland and his team continued to promote the festival, driven by the desire to secure more funding and maintain public interest.

The unraveling of the Fyre Festival began in April 2017, when attendees arrived to find a poorly organized and under-resourced event. Instead of the promised luxury accommodations, guests were met with disaster relief tents and inadequate facilities. The gourmet meals were replaced with basic sandwiches, and many musical acts pulled out at the last minute.

Legal and financial consequences swiftly followed, with McFarland and his team facing multiple lawsuits and criminal charges. McFarland was eventually sentenced to six years in prison for wire fraud, and the financial fallout left many investors and ticket buyers with significant losses.

The impact on attendees and stakeholders was profound. Many guests, who had paid thousands of dollars for the experience, were left stranded and disappointed. The scandal also led to a broader crisis of confidence in influencer marketing and event planning.

The Fyre Festival fraud prompted significant scrutiny of social media marketing practices and event planning standards. The scandal exposed the risks associated with influencer marketing and highlighted the need for greater transparency and accountability.

Long-term consequences for the event planning industry included increased emphasis on due diligence and more rigorous planning processes. The scandal also underscored the importance of ethical marketing practices and the need for honesty in promotional materials.

Analysis of the scandal's legacy reveals that while it served as a wake-up call for the industry, challenges remain. The lessons from the Fyre Festival continue to be relevant as marketers and event planners navigate the complexities of social media and consumer expectations.

The Fyre Festival fraud serves as a stark reminder of the dangers of overhyped promises and inadequate planning. By understanding the factors that led to the festival's collapse, we can better appreciate the need for transparency, accountability, and ethical marketing practices. The story of the Fyre Festival remains a cautionary tale for event planners and marketers alike, emphasizing the enduring relevance of integrity and oversight.

Chapter 20: The Charles Keating and Lincoln Savings and Loan Scandal (1989)

The Charles Keating and Lincoln Savings and Loan scandal, one of the most prominent cases of financial fraud in the late 20th century, had far-reaching implications for the banking industry and regulatory oversight. This book explores the rise and fall of Lincoln Savings and Loan, the fraudulent practices that led to its collapse, and the broader implications for financial regulation.

Lincoln Savings and Loan, under the leadership of Charles Keating, became a symbol of the excesses and abuses of the Savings and Loan (S&L) industry in the 1980s. Keating's aggressive business strategies and close political connections allowed him to expand Lincoln's operations rapidly, attracting significant investment and attention.

The economic and regulatory environment of the 1980s, characterized by deregulation and a booming real estate market, provided a backdrop for Lincoln's growth. The relaxation of regulatory oversight allowed S&Ls to engage in riskier activities, setting the stage for widespread abuses.

Key figures involved in the scandal included Charles Keating, Lincoln's CEO; and a group of U.S. Senators, later known as the "Keating Five," who were implicated in efforts to protect Keating from regulatory scrutiny. These individuals played crucial roles in the events leading up to the scandal.

Lincoln Savings and Loan's fraudulent practices centered on high-risk investments and the misappropriation of funds. Keating used Lincoln's resources to finance speculative real estate ventures and personal projects, diverting funds from their intended purposes.

The manipulation of financial statements and regulatory reports allowed Lincoln to present a misleading picture of financial health. The company's aggressive lobbying efforts, bolstered by political contributions and personal relationships, helped shield it from regulatory intervention.

Stories from within the organization reveal a culture of greed and complicity. Many employees were pressured to engage in unethical practices, and regulatory officials were often influenced or intimidated into overlooking irregularities.

The unraveling of Lincoln Savings and Loan began in the late 1980s, when the Federal Home Loan Bank Board (FHLBB) initiated investigations into the company's activities. The discovery of widespread fraud and mismanagement led to Lincoln's eventual seizure by regulators in 1989.

Legal and financial consequences swiftly followed, with Keating facing multiple charges of fraud, racketeering, and conspiracy. He was eventually convicted and sentenced to prison, although his convictions were partially overturned on appeal.

The impact on investors and the public was significant. Thousands of investors, many of them elderly, lost their savings, and the collapse of Lincoln contributed to the broader Savings and Loan Crisis. The scandal also led to increased scrutiny of political contributions and regulatory oversight.

The Charles Keating and Lincoln Savings and Loan scandal prompted significant regulatory changes aimed at preventing similar occurrences in the future. The Financial Institutions Reform, Recovery, and Enforcement Act (FIRREA) of 1989 introduced stringent requirements for financial reporting, internal controls, and regulatory oversight.

Long-term consequences for the financial industry included greater emphasis on transparency and accountability. The scandal underscored the importance of ethical leadership and the need for effective regulatory frameworks to protect investors and the public.

Analysis of the scandal's legacy reveals that while regulatory reforms have strengthened oversight, challenges remain. The lessons from Lincoln Savings and Loan continue to be relevant as the financial industry navigates the complexities of modern markets.

The Charles Keating and Lincoln Savings and Loan scandal serves as a powerful reminder of the dangers of unchecked greed and the importance of robust regulatory frameworks. By understanding the factors that led to Lincoln's downfall, we can better appreciate the need for ethical leadership and strong governance in the financial world. The story of Lincoln Savings and Loan remains a cautionary tale for the banking industry and regulators alike, emphasizing the enduring relevance of integrity and accountability.

About the Author

About the Author

Linda Carrol, a native of rural Biloxi, Mississippi, discovered her passion for storytelling amidst the quiet beauty of her Southern surroundings. With her closest neighbor miles away, Linda sought solace and adventure within the pages of beloved books by authors such as J.K. Rowling, Frances Hodgson Burnett, and Michael Ende.

Armed with a degree in education from Mississippi State University, Linda embarked on a fulfilling career as an elementary school teacher. However, her love for literature and her desire to ignite the imaginations of young minds led her down a new path.

Fueled by a deep-seated passion for children's literature, Linda made the bold decision to transition from teaching to writing, channeling the enchanting storytelling styles of her literary heroes into her own work. Since then, she has emerged as one of Mississippi's most prolific writers, captivating readers with her vivid imagination, Southern charm, and heartfelt narratives.

Linda's dedication to fostering a love of reading and creativity in children extends beyond the written page. Through workshops, school visits, and community outreach programs, she continues to inspire young readers to explore new worlds and discover the magic of storytelling.

Recipient of multiple awards, including two Silver Kite Awards and the prestigious Moonlight Award, Linda Carrol's work resonates with readers of all ages, transporting them to enchanting realms where imagination knows no bounds.

Join Linda on a journey through the pages of her enchanting stories, where every tale is infused with the warmth of the South and the timeless joy of childhood wonder.